FANTASTIC folders and EXCEPTIONAL envelopes

A DESIGNER'S GUIDE TO CUSTOM CARRIERS THAT OPEN CONVERSATIONS AND SEAL DEALS

PATRICIA BELYEA | JENNY SULLIVAN

GLOUCESTER MASSACHUSETTS

ROCKPORT PUBLISHERS

First published in the United States of America by

Rockport Publishers, a member of
Quayside Publishing Group
33 Commercial Street
Gloucester, Massachusetts 01930-5089
Telephone: (978) 282-9590
Fax: (978) 283-2742
www.rockpub.com

Library of Congress Cataloging-in-Publication Data

Belyea, Patricia.
    Fantastic folders and exceptional envelopes: a designer's guide to
custom carriers that open conversations and seal deals / Patricia
Belyea and Jenny Sullivan.
       p. cm.

    ISBN-13: 978-1-59253-175-2
    ISBN-10: 1-59253-175-X (pbk.)
    1. Packaging—Handbooks, manuals, etc. 2. Commercial art.
I. Sullivan, Jenny, [date] II. Title.
  TS195.B45 2005
  769.56'6—dc22   2005004669
                                CIP

10 9 8 7 6 5 4 3 2

Design: Belyea

Printed in China

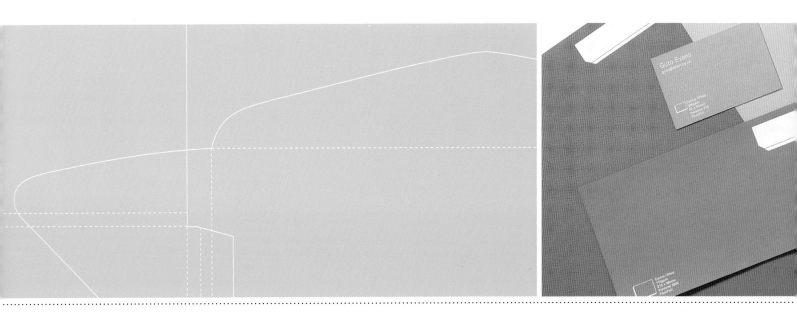

To Michael, who encourages me to be me. To Ron, who allows me to get carried away. And to Liz and Vik, who love me even when I do not pick them up on time.

Acknowledgments My thanks to:
Jenny Sullivan, my relentless and dear writing partner;
Naomi Murphy, the lead architect and designer of the book;
Kristin Ellison, who bolstered and guided us patiently;
The folks at Graphic Impressions and Seattle Envelope who graciously educated me on the finer points of production details;
Designers around the world who shipped large packages and responded to all my questions;
The team at Belyea who birthed this book while juggling many more responsibilities;
And my family, who allowed me to ignore them again and again.

PB

CONTENTS

A soup-to-nuts primer on the rules of folder design, how to break them, and what happens to your job once it's in production, from die cutting to scoring to folding to gluing. Learn how to troubleshoot common pitfalls and partner effectively with printers and finishers. Plus, check out helpful tips on specifying papers and embellishments that command attention.

Everything you ever wanted to know about envelope styles, adhesives, closures, and manufacturing. Understand how to partner with conversion houses to create one-of-a-kind masterpieces, and heed some words to the wise on postal regulations and other factors that can make or break a stellar envelope design.

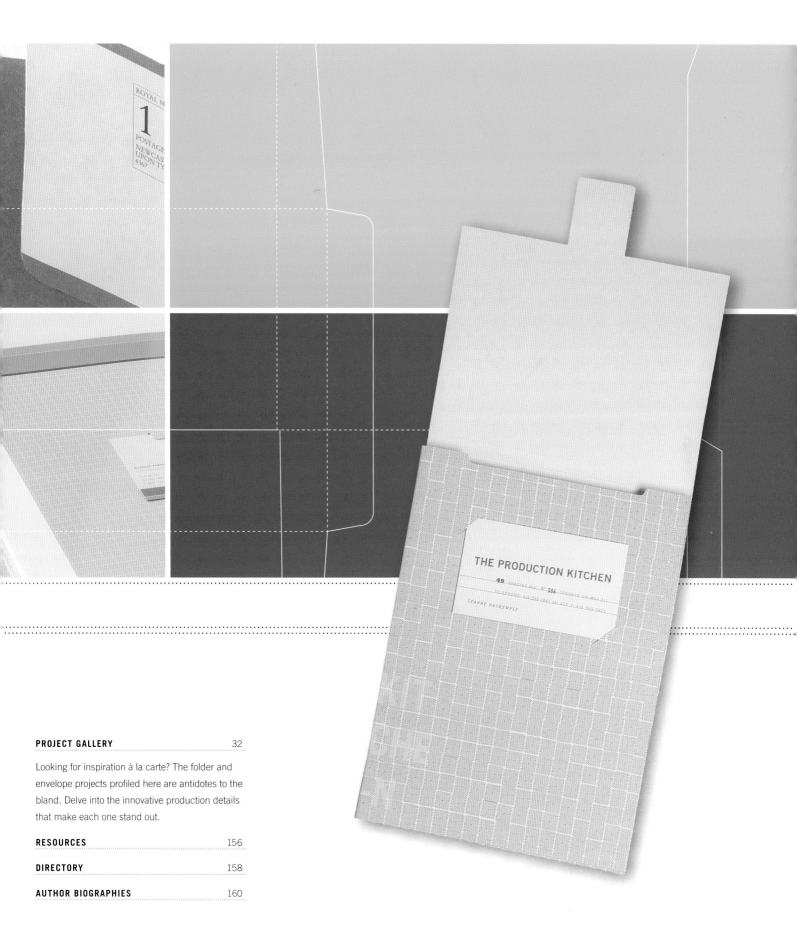

INTRODUCTION

Care Packages Never Go Out of Style

Who needs a paper folder or plastic envelope in the age of digital communication? Why not attach that important announcement or irresistible proposal to an email that lands right on the recipient's desktop?

We all know the answer to this question. Email abuse, from misguided "reply all" posts to prolific spam, has made us less than excited when messages pile up in our electronic mailboxes. Even smart, well-targeted online promos feel impersonal. Wearied by our allegiance to the mouse and monitor, we have renewed our craving for parcels that are tactile, substantive, and special.

As designers, we are charged with creating results. This book is meant to help you achieve them. Under the right circumstances, a jaw-dropping folder or envelope that is as compelling as its contents will catapult a client to a new level of recognition. But breaking the rules effectively requires an intimate understanding of the manufacturing steps that will transform your vision from idea to reality.

In the pages that follow, you'll find practical information on the processes and materials essential to folder- and envelope-making, plus real-world examples of carriers that superseded the status quo. A portfolio gallery of ambitious projects from around the world offers first-hand insights and production tips from seasoned designers.

Think of the gallery as a starting point. Perhaps you'll find inspiration in an unorthodox pocket style, an interesting use of paper, a fun set of business card slots, or an unusual fastener. What you derive from it is up to you.

There is just one immutable law governing the world of folders and envelopes: Be sure to partner with the best vendors. They will engineer your job so it is produced to the highest standards while being cost-effective.

Go, design and thrive.

Producing a distinctive folder requires remarkable design and attention to many **production details.**

Standard 9" X 12" (22.5 X 30 cm) folders with horizontal pockets are everywhere. In this sea of sameness, an impeccably designed and cleverly shaped folder tailored to hold a custom set of materials makes a powerful impression. But a smart design concept is only half of the equation. Equally important is for every production detail to be shrewdly premeditated, pretested, and well executed.

Before you start designing, think about how and where your folder will be used. What will it hold? How many pockets will be required? Will it need extra capacity for bulky items such as booklets or CDs? How will the contents be presented inside the folder? Will the folder mail in an envelope or other carrier? Will it be used as a handout at meetings or trade shows? How much handling and abuse will it need to

withstand? Will it complement other marketing collateral within a larger design system? The answers to these questions will begin to shape your design and production parameters.

Die cutting 101

Folders start as flat templates that must be die-cut, scored, folded, and glued. A die board is a piece of wood outfitted with steel rules, resembling a giant cookie cutter, mounted on a piece of plywood. Rule blades may be sharp (for cutting), dull (for scoring) or gapped (for perforating). Rules protrude from die boards at different heights, depending on whether they are intended to cut through the paper or to merely press into the paper to score it for folding.

Like printing, die-cutting is often accomplished by feeding paper through a press. In lieu of a printing plate, however, the paper comes into contact with the die board and is cut and/or scored. Today's die-cutting presses can be calibrated to within $1/100$" (0.03 cm) for a precise cut.

There are two types of presses used for die-cutting folders. In a flatbed cylinder press, the die is anchored on a flat surface underneath the cylinder. The paper wraps around the cylinder that rolls over the die. The other option is a platen press, in which the paper sheet is fed through the press flat. In addition to die-cutting, a platen press can be modified to foil stamp, emboss, or deboss. A platen press is the clear choice for rigid substrates, such as board stock, that do not easily bend.

Various die sets are used to fabricate die-cutting rules into all shapes and sizes.

Rubber "ejectors" create a spring effect and help to push the die away from the cut paper, thus preventing snags. The ejection rubber sits about $1/16"$ (0.16 cm) higher than the cutting rule.

A sign of sound craftsmanship: joints where die blades meet should be mitered so that one rule fits over the bevel of another. This helps to avoid an imperfect corner cut that can tear the paper.

A jigsaw or laser etches the pattern (dieline) into the wooden dieboard. Cutting and scoring rules made of steel are then pounded into the channels in the dieboard with a rawhide mallet by a die maker.

GOING PLATEN

Ninety percent of the time, a platen press is used for full-perimeter die-cutting, and for jobs in which each single press sheet holds more than one folder template. Set up times for platen presses are typically longer than for cylinder presses.

Working with Printers and Finishers

Some commercial printers offer folder die-cutting and assembly in-house. More often than not, though, a printer will subcontract these tasks to an outside vendor, often referred to as a trade print finisher or impression shop.

By the time a folder project lands in the hands of a finisher, it has probably already been printed. The finishing shop engineers the necessary steps to convert each folder from flat to dimensional form. This includes the creation of die boards for cutting, scoring, and perforating. In addition, the finisher may offer other postproduction services such as embossing or debossing, foil stamping, letterpress, engraving, UV coating, film/paper laminating, and hand detailing. Two capabilities that finishing shops generally don't offer are paper procurement and fulfillment.

Is it a good idea to bypass a printer and contract directly with a finisher? Generally, no—just as you wouldn't circumvent a building contractor to bring in an outside drywall installer in the midst of a home remodeling project. A printer that has an established rapport with a finisher will have more leverage in expediting tight time frames and demanding reruns if there are quality problems. And to the extent that folder assembly is an intermediary step in a process that will most likely begin and end with the printer, it's best to let the printer manage the project all the way through.

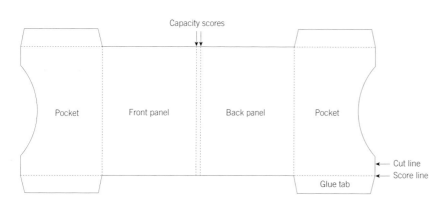

Capacity scores

| Pocket | Front panel | Back panel | Pocket |

Cut line
Score line

Glue tab

Anatomy of a Folder

The folder dieline has two different types of lines on it. Solid lines denote cuts and dashed lines denote folds. The width of the spine is determined by the distance between capacity scores in the middle of the folder, less the thickness of the paper. (A folder without added capacity will have a single score down the middle.) Here, a concave die-cut produces an interesting pocket shape.

COUNTRY	USA
DESIGN FIRM	Belyea
CREATIVE DIRECTOR	Patricia Belyea
DESIGNER	Anne Dougherty
CLIENT	K/P Corporation
PRINTER	K/P Corporation

Nevertheless, understanding the mechanics of how folders are created can work to your advantage.

Paper Choices

Paper choice will have both aesthetic and practical repercussions. Will you go with a coated stock for a smooth, shiny finish, or an uncoated sheet that is soft to the touch and perhaps sports an interesting texture? There are advantages and disadvantages to both options. Coated surfaces, for example, need a final finish such as a varnish to minimize fingerprints. Uncoated stocks are less water resistant.

Duplex stock can be a great choice for folders. Constructed of two paper stocks glued together, duplex stocks are very sturdy. Some paper mills offer premade duplex stocks in contrasting colors. This allows a folder to feature one color on the outside and another on the inside. Although duplex stocks are made with two sheets of cover weight paper, they are still lightweight enough for lithographic printing. You can also make your own duplex stock by working with a paper laminator.

Today's laminators can glue printed papers together accurately so they back up perfectly. While premade duplexes are always made with the same type of paper on each side, custom duplexes can be made with contrasting stocks, such as a gloss sheet on one side and an uncoated stock on the other. The lamination stage may take place before or after printing, depending on how your printer engineers the job.

Noncapacity and Capacity Folders

Here are noncapacity and capacity versions of a folder with horizontal pockets. The spine and pocket tabs in the capacity folder are double-scored to create a three-dimensional holding area for inserts.

Noncapacity folder   Capacity folder

Flap Tabs and Body Tabs

There are different kinds of glue tabs, as evidenced by these dielines for a folder with vertical pockets. Body tabs protrude from the main body of the folder. Flap tabs extend from the flaps that will fold inward to create pockets.

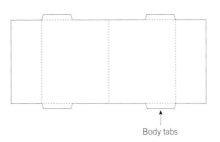 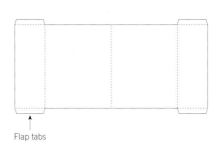

Body tabs   Flap tabs

COOL MAY NOT COST MORE

If you plan to have a custom die created for your folder project, a uniquely shaped die won't necessarily cost more than a traditional one. Take advantage of the opportunity to think creatively and explore your options with your printer or impression shop.

Folder Details

A folder template is called a dieline. If your piece includes glued pockets, the dieline pattern will need to incorporate glue tabs. Glue tabs should be at least ¾" (2 cm) wide, as narrower tabs are not easy to glue.

Slots and Notches

Cuts in the folder pockets can be engineered to hold items such as small brochures, CDs, or business cards. These slots can be cut in a variety of shapes to create interesting positive/negative spatial relationships.

Closures

If your folder is unlikely to lie flat once it's stuffed, you'll need some sort of clasp or closure to hold everything together. Depending on the girth of your piece, you may be able to wrap things up by designing a special paper tab and slot that lock together. Alternative closures may incorporate Velcro dots, elastic bands, rubber bands, plastic snaps, ribbons, grommets, or button-and-string combinations. Many closures will require hand assembly, but this unique touch can be worth the expense.

A creative clasp or clever closure can provide the perfect finishing touch to an eye-catching piece.

FROM TOP LEFT:
Paper tab closure, snap closure, paper belly band, wide rubber band, button-and-string style closure incorporating ribbon in lieu of string, elastic band with notched guides

A GALLERY OF BUSINESS CARD SLOTS

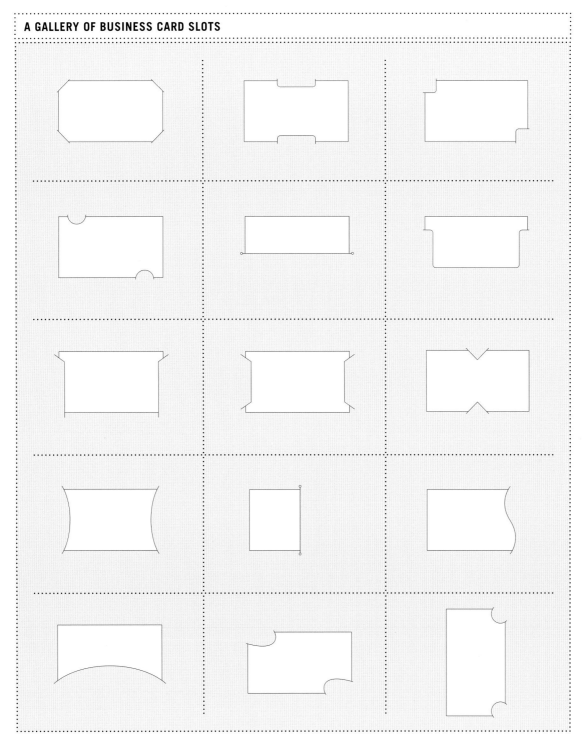

Radius Corners

Rounded corners or curved folder pockets can be a nice departure from the norm. Radius corners can be die-cut in one of two ways, each with its own compromise.

Option one is to create a single die board that makes a full perimeter die-cut in one press pass. To ensure that the die-cut section of the paper stays attached to the main sheet as it moves through the press (preventing the scrap from falling out and jamming the press), the curved parts of the cutting rule are nicked so that the cut is interrupted. The little pieces of paper that bridge the die-cut are called "ties." When the sheet reaches the end of the press, a stripping tool breaks the ties and punches out the scrap. As a result, little tufts of paper may stick out in the spots where the ties were broken. The good news is that nicks in the cutting blade can be made as small as $8/1000"$ (0.01 mm), so the little hangnails left by broken ties are nearly imperceptible.

Option two is to cut the curves first with a stand-alone die rule and then cut the straight sides with a guillotine straight edge. The downside to this approach is that the straight edges are cut in stacks (called lifts) and the paper will shift slightly as the guillotine blade cuts through the stack. That means some rounded corners will not match perfectly to the straight edge. This shifting problem can be minimized by trimming shorter lifts (smaller piles).

Full Perimeter Die-cut

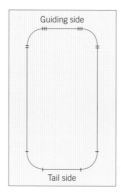

Breaks in the cutting blades keep the product in place while die-cutting.

Breaks in the cutting dies create "ties".

Finished product is punched out of the press sheet.

Nonperimeter Die-cut

Die-cut four corners and two sides.

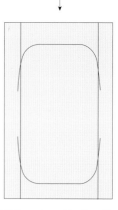

Guillotine cut remaining two sides.

Finished product.

To Glue or Not to Glue?

Most folder pockets are assembled with discreet tabs that are tucked under and glued. Gluing is done by hand or by machine, depending on the quantity and complexity of the job. Hand gluing is often specified for small projects that do not warrant the set-up time and expense of a gluing machine. Hand gluing may also be necessary if the job is too complex to automate. For example, boxed or capacity pockets cannot be machine glued.

Your printer or finishing shop will determine the best glue for your project, choosing among the following adhesive options:

Cold melt glue is applied as a liquid on an automatic folding machine. Because this glue dries by evaporation, it tends to stay wet longer and requires time and pressure to set. Beware that cold glue can sometimes soak through a particularly lightweight stock and stain the paper. For this reason, it's a good idea to consult with your printer or finisher early on when you are choosing the paper for your folder project. Cold melt glue is cheaper than hot melt glue, and is the glue used most often for folder projects.

Hot melt glue hardens as it cools. It can be applied by machine or by hand, and is one of the strongest adhesives available. Hot melt glue

is used for projects with surfaces that are difficult to glue due to their finish, weight, or thickness. It is often used to fortify panels that might have a tendency to spring apart.

Double-sided tape is always applied by hand with a triggered tape gun. It is often the adhesive of choice for short-run projects that don't warrant the set up of an automated gluing machine. Double-sided tape may also be used on capacity folders that cannot be assembled automatically or in instances where liquid glue is likely to stain the paper.

There are also ways to design a folder without a glued pocket. In a multipanel configuration, the center panel has a flap that folds up and the outside panels fold inward to hold the folder's contents in place. Nonglued pockets can also be made from flaps that fold over one another and interlock.

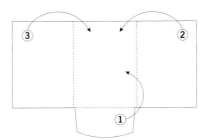

Three-panel folder with nonglued pocket flap

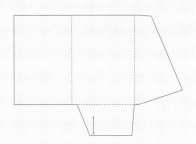

This folder delivers high impact on a low budget. To avoid gluing expenses, the two inside flaps were designed to lock together to create a holding area. A translucent stock allows the printing on the inside flap to show through the cover, adding a second dimension to the headline.

COUNTRY	USA
DESIGN FIRM	Belyea
CREATIVE DIRECTOR	Patricia Belyea
DESIGNER	Ron Lars Hansen
CLIENT	Linna Photographics
PRINTER	Olympus Press

Troubleshooting with Dummies

The template for a die-cut is called a dieline. Some designers will create a dieline as a layer in Adobe Illustrator (or similar software) and send the art to the printer/finisher as a guide. Even if you do this, it's a good idea to also construct a paper dummy and test your folder concept with its proposed contents before you send the job to the printer. This physical exercise will help you refine the structure of your folder and troubleshoot any sizing issues. Plus, the paper dummy, however crude, will be helpful in articulating your vision so the printer can prepare an accurate price estimate.

Ideally, you'll want to work with a vendor with CAD capabilities. Unlike your hand-cut dummy, a CAD dummy can be made to exact specifications. A dieline made in the shop with a CAD machine will cut an actual

sample from the paper you plan to use to manufacture your folder. This is a premium service that adds a couple hundred dollars to a job, but it's worth it.

During the design phase, ask your printer or finisher to generate three CAD dummies: one for their files, one for your client, and one for your own reference. The dummies will come in handy when you need to discuss the project with the client or finishing shop and can't meet face to face.

To create a CAD dummy, your finisher will need an actual paper sample or at least the specs on your paper's thickness (texture does not make a difference). A CAD dummy is a wonderful tool for ensuring the viability of your folder design before the entire job goes under the blade. Use the CAD dummy to test your

business card slots, pockets, and inserts once again and make sure they fit the way you expect them to. It may seem redundant, but this live test can preempt disaster. If your paper choice is too light, your dummy will feel floppy and flimsy. If your paper is too bulky, your contents may not slide into the pockets as easily as you'd anticipated.

If your CAD dummy reveals unforeseen problems, you can make adjustments to your design before it's too late. Just be sure to alert your printer of any revised paper specifications, as a change in the paper thickness will necessitate a refinement of the dieline. Also, be aware that any new paper (and subsequently a new dieline) may slightly alter the placement of your graphics. You'll want to revisit the artwork to make sure everything is placed correctly before the job goes to prepress.

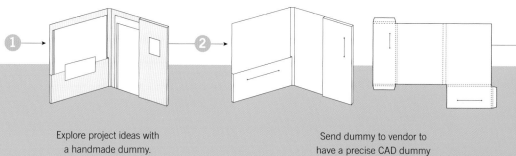

From start to finish, perfect folders are the product of ingenuity and due diligence. Here's a snapshot of each step in the folder production process.

Explore project ideas with a handmade dummy.

Send dummy to vendor to have a precise CAD dummy and dieline produced.

COUNTRY	USA
DESIGN FIRM	Belyea
CREATIVE DIRECTOR	Patricia Belyea
DESIGNER	Naomi Murphy
CLIENT	Fraser Papers
PRINTER	K/P Corporation

Multiple full-scale dummies helped refine the engineering of this complex folder. The corrugated cover was debossed for the inset, and the entire folder was die-cut on a platen press. The letterpressed, die-cut flower inset was hand glued with hot melt glue. The barb of the elastic cord closure was fed through a hole in the back and then secured on the inside with a clear label. The left inside panel was taped along the top and gutter, and then secured with hot melt glue along the bottom seam to ensure bulky inserts did not pull the seal open. The right inside panel was folded and glued along the top, bottom, and gutter with double-sided tape.

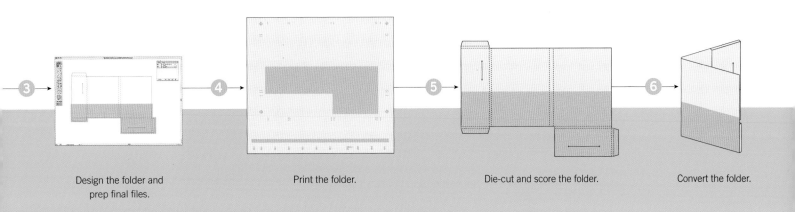

③ Design the folder and prep final files.

④ Print the folder.

⑤ Die-cut and score the folder.

⑥ Convert the folder.

Common Pitfalls

Most folder fiascoes can be avoided with fore-thought, planning, and solid communication between designer, printer, and finisher. Here are some common pitfalls and how to avoid them.

Cracking Cracking is a common problem on stock with heavy ink coverage. When cracking occurs along scored edges, the white paper pulp beneath the surface of the ink shows through. To avoid cracking, consider adding a protective coating such as aqueous, varnish, or spot UV, and fold in the direction of the paper grain (if possible). Your finisher may also use "counters" during scoring as a preemptive measure. A counter is a cushion that supports the underside of the paper when the scoring rule is applied. The counter softens the blow of the scoring blade, thereby lessening the likelihood that the edge of the score will split. If you specify a coated stock, ask your printer or finisher to be extra vigilant about wraparounds (scored, folded edges with heavy ink coverage).

Tearing Die-cut slots that are intended to hold heavy items, such as CDs or fat booklets, can sometimes tear at the ends. A round pinhole on either side of the die-cut will help prevent the opening from tearing.

Glue Glitches For maximum adhesion, tab surfaces should be left unprinted and unvarnished. A folder tab coated with varnish will not stick well to another varnished surface. Be sure to design your folder so there is no ink or varnish on the areas that need to be glued. If you are unsure where to "knock out" the art, ask your printer to adjust your digital files in the prepress stage.

Capacity Issues When it comes to folders, one size does not fit all. A folder needs to hold its contents snugly or the pieces will jostle around and look messy. Capacity folders with boxed pockets and double-scored spines should be produced only when bulky inserts require the extra room. If the quantity or thickness of the inserts will vary, you may want to design and produce two matching folders for your client—one that is flat and the other with capacity.

Bent Pockets Pockets should never run flush against the spine of the folder. If they do, it will be impossible to close the folder without bending the pocket corners. The necessary gap between the inside edge of the pocket and the spine is called relief. The general rule is this: the thicker the folder capacity, the wider the relief. Pockets are generally tapered at an angle to keep the corners from becoming dog-eared.

SHOPPING FOR THE RIGHT PARTNER

Here are some questions to ask when choosing a printer and/or trade finisher:

> Does the printer offer one-stop shopping, with folder capabilities in-house? If so, what kind of equipment do they use? If not, where will the work be subcontracted? Ask to see samples of other folder projects they've managed or executed.

> Can the printer or finisher provide a CAD-generated dummy before the job goes on press? This will be critical for pretesting your folder concept. (For more on CAD dummies, see pages 16 and 17.)

> Does the printer or finisher offer automated (in addition to manual) folding and gluing? If so, will your project qualify for machine work, or will the nature of the job necessitate hand assembly?

> Can the printer or finisher handle other embellishments that have been specified (such as foil stamping or embossing) or will these steps need to be farmed out to another subcontractor? The more vendors involved, the longer the time frame. Outsourcing may also increase the price of the job as the printer will mark up the costs of the additional vendors' services.

> Will you have the opportunity to visit the finishing shop for a die check? This may be key if your job involves experimental techniques or unorthodox fabrication materials. The more opportunities you have to interact with the craftsmen who are engineering your project, the easier it will be to tweak, troubleshoot, and prevent costly mistakes.

Unwanted Impressions If your cover is embossed, debossed, or engraved, remember the same dimensional shape will appear in reverse on the inside. One cloaking solution is to incorporate an extra panel that folds over and is glued to create a double-thick front cover. Another option is to position the art so that the back of the impression is hidden by one of the inside pockets.

Waste Are you limited to running one folder per press sheet, or can you nest two or more to a sheet to save money and paper? If it's a close call, talk to your printer about whether the project can be slightly resized to gain efficiencies on the press sheet.

Shipping Snafus No folder job is complete until the finished items reach their final destination undamaged. If your folders are packed snugly

into cartons and delivered across town, they should arrive in good shape. For long-distance trucking, the cartons should be loaded onto pallets. Shipping via delivery companies warrants careful packing and extra padding since items are more likely to be jostled around in the belly of a plane or the untethered cabin of a tractor trailer. In this case, capacity folders may fare better if they are supported by cardboard fillers that help maintain their shape.

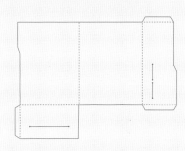

Die-cut edges on the cover and inside pocket of this folder playfully evoke the look of file folders. The business cards are cut in the same staggered shape. This folder was die-cut on a platen press and finished on an automated folder/gluer. Although it looks like a standard job, it had to be printed a second time and die-cut with a reengineered die due to excessive cracking (see page 18) along the bottom inside pocket corners.

COUNTRY	USA
DESIGN FIRM	Belyea
CREATIVE DIRECTOR	Patricia Belyea
DESIGNER	Ron Lars Hansen
CLIENT	K/P Corporation
PRINTER	K/P Corporation

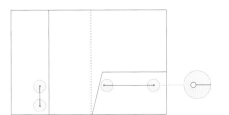

Slots with Pinholes
Round pinholes at either end of a die-cut slot will prevent the edges from tearing.

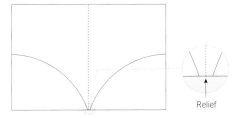

Relief Space
Relief space on either side of the folder's center seam ensures that the piece will close easily and lie flat without bunching or buckling.

A dynamic envelope can do more than deliver its contents. It can generate excitement and memorability.

Envelopes are often treated as an afterthought, but they shouldn't be. An unusual envelope can make a savvy addition to a business paper system, a dazzling direct mail piece that gets opened and acted upon, or a memorable jacket for a keepsake announcement. Creating a custom envelope from scratch affords more creativity than settling for what's available in stores and catalogs. Perhaps the envelope you envision has graphics wrapping from front to back. Maybe the flap is a unique shape with an expressive edge and the inside is printed a vibrant color. Maybe the envelope isn't made of paper at all but, rather, of translucent plastic.

Breaking convention can be very effective, as long as you don't abandon functionality. Will your envelope transport materials via postal mail or messenger services? What will it hold and how heavy will the contents be? If mailings are planned, will the pieces be addressed by hand, fed through a laser printer, or affixed with peel-and-stick address labels? Contemplating these and other key factors ahead of time can prevent costly mistakes, not to mention ulcers.

Anatomy of an Envelope

A flat envelope pattern (called a dieline) shows the placement of glue flaps that will eventually be folded over and sealed to create a pocket. Solid lines denote cuts, whereas dashed lines indicate seams that will be scored and folded.

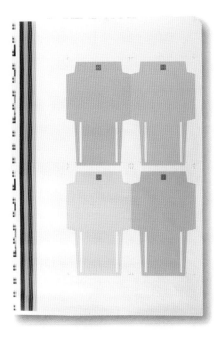

Envelopes can be ganged up on a single press sheet to get the most mileage out of your paper and budget.

COUNTRY	USA
DESIGN FIRM	Belyea
CREATIVE DIRECTOR	Patricia Belyea
DESIGNER	Ben Reynolds
CLIENT	Belyea
PRINTER	ColorGraphics

Here, CMYK printing allows for a system of envelopes with different color interiors for the same cost as one color interior.

Envelope Details

Envelope templates are based on one of three configurations: side seam, center seam, or diagonal seam.

(1) Top flap or seal flap

(2) Face

(3) Side flap

(4) Back flap or bottom flap

Side seam

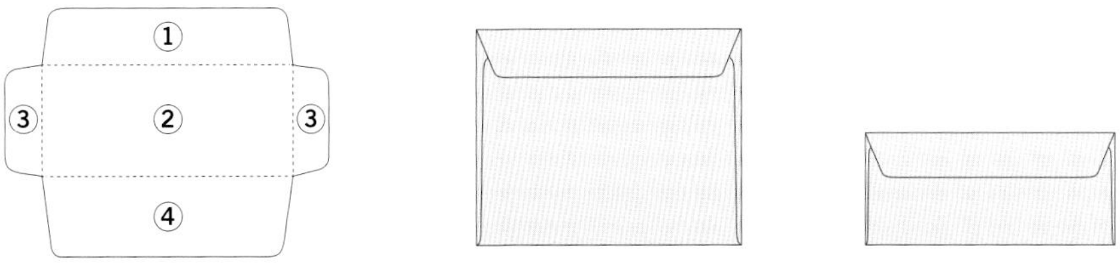

Center seam

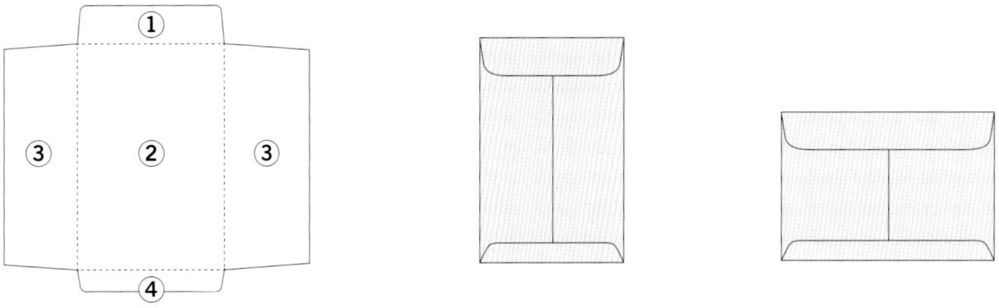

Diagonal seam

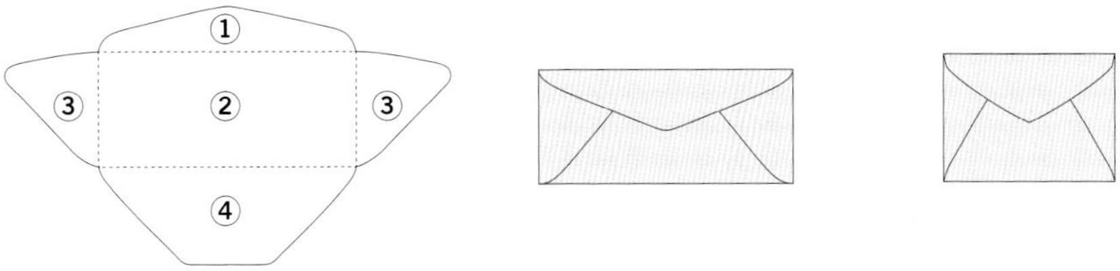

Envelope flaps come in different styles. The shape of the flap can affect the final look and paper efficiency of the envelope package. If you cannot find what you want, customize a flap that works with your design.

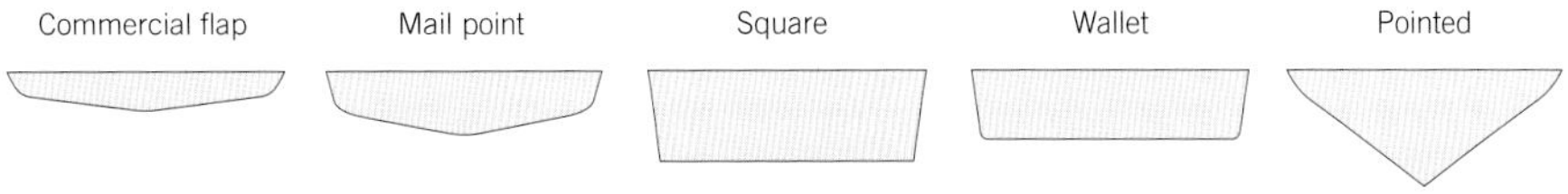

Commercial flap

Mail point

Square

Wallet

Pointed

The Art of Conversion

Like folders, envelopes start out as flat templates that are then cut, scored, folded, and glued to create an enclosure. The act of taking a flat sheet of paper and turning it into an envelope is called conversion. Big commercial printers may offer conversion services in-house, but most subcontract to conversion shops specializing in envelope manufacturing. Here's a quick overview of how envelopes are made:

1. Flat sheets of paper are printed with the graphics you've designed.

2. The press sheets are transported to the conversion shop, where they are cut into flat shapes, known as blanks. Blanks may be created by feeding the press sheets through a die-cutting press (if a full-perimeter cut is required), or they can be cut with a cookie-cutter type die known as a closed die or steel die. For small runs or odd-sized envelopes, an adjustable die may be used. An adjustable die is a system of movable blades that can be calibrated to match the size of the envelope face and seal flap.

3. Blanks are fed into an industrial converting machine that scores, folds, and glues the envelopes together mechanically. In special circumstances, blanks may be converted by hand.

Paper Choices

Designing a custom envelope that is both attractive and functional requires a bit of forethought, and paper is a major consideration.

Aesthetics notwithstanding, there may be usage constraints. If the envelopes will be addressed by feeding them through a laser printer, the stock you choose should be light enough to not cause jamming. Most office printers can accommodate business envelopes made of 24W (60T) or 28W (70T) paper. If the envelope will hold heavy or bulky items, it will need to be made of a durable material that won't tear under stress. Address labels may not stick well to a highly textured surface. If the address will appear on the envelope proper (not on a label), you may need to avoid a dark paper stock. And, of course, there are postal regulations that will influence your paper choice if you plan to use the mail system. These are highlighted in more detail on pages 24–26.

Not all envelopes are converted in a machine. This example was die-cut and scored, then glued by hand. The cost per unit was higher than a machine-converted envelope, but handwork was a smart choice in light of the unusual design and cover-weight stock. Because this envelope was not intended for mailing purposes, it was allowed to remain open at the top.

COUNTRY	USA
DESIGN FIRM	Belyea
CREATIVE DIRECTOR	Patricia Belyea
DESIGNER	Naomi Murphy
CLIENT	Evan Goetzmann
PRINTER	Artcraft Printing

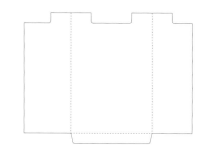

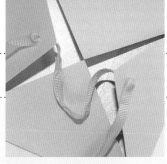

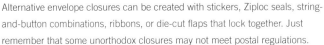

Alternative envelope closures can be created with stickers, Ziploc seals, string-and-button combinations, ribbons, or die-cut flaps that lock together. Just remember that some unorthodox closures may not meet postal regulations.

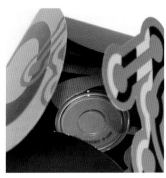

Adhesives and Closures

There are two families of adhesives in the envelope equation. One is used to glue the seams of the envelope; the other is used on the seal flap. Your printer or converter will decide which type of glue is best to hold the seams closed in light of the dimensions and paper you've specified.

For the seal flap, there are several glue options. The best choice will depend on your intended use.

Lick-and-stick glue is an inexpensive, remoistenable glue that is applied in automated machines as an in-line process. The glue starts as a liquid, dries, and then requires water (or saliva) to seal. Hence its name. The downside to this glue is that the remoistening process can be messy for the end user. Excess water leaking from sponge-tipped applicators may drip onto other parts of the envelope, or cause the edges of the flap to buckle.

Latex glue is similar in consistency to rubber cement. This option requires the application of two lines of adhesive—one on the seal flap and the other on the body of the envelope. The two lines of adhesive form a bond when they are pressed together. This glue is used exclusively for hand sealing jobs. Because latex glue is a nonaggressive sealant, the envelope flap can be opened and resealed rather easily without damaging the envelope. Latex glue stays sticky for one year. The best glue for the job may be determined by how quickly your envelopes will be used.

Peel-and-seal adhesive is a more expensive choice for a waterless seal. It consists of a pressure-sensitive tape that comes with a protective strip on top. Once the liner strip is removed, the flap with the tape is pressed closed. Machines can be used to apply peel-and-seal adhesive in huge quantities, but usually the tape is applied off-line (by hand). Peel-and-seal adhesive remains sticky for about two years.

There are also alternatives to glue. These may include string-and-button and clasp closures, which can be applied by machines at major converting shops. Standard buttons, strings, and grommets come in a limited number of colors and finishes for envelopes.

DIE REUSE?

If your concept calls for a special shaped envelope, check with your finisher to find out if they already have a die that closely resembles the die you need. If so, you can save some dollars by using a preexisting die instead of requiring the finisher to fabricate a new one.

Postage Matters

Will your envelopes be mailed? If so, this may have a big impact on your design parameters. The size, weight, shape, and content of each mail piece will affect your postage costs. Furthermore, postal services in most countries maintain strict regulations regarding the physical properties of correspondence sent by mail.

United States

In the United States, requirements are especially stringent if you want your envelope to qualify for automated processing, which saves time and money. Your design will need to adhere to certain standards to make sure it can sail through processing equipment that moves mail at a speed of up to 40,000 pieces per hour. Envelopes that are "nonmachinable" are subject to a surcharge because they must be processed manually. Some factors that may render a first-class, letter-size envelope "nonmachinable" in the United States include:

Dimensions Envelopes that are taller than 6 1/16" (15.5 cm), longer than 11 1/2" (29 cm), or thicker than 1/4" (0.6 cm) must be processed by hand.

Shape Square and other unorthodox envelope dimensions can jam automated equipment and must be manually processed.

Heft Envelopes that are too flimsy may stick together or get caught in the metal joints of the processing equipment. Pieces that are too rigid and don't bend easily will have a harder time navigating tight conveyor belt turns without getting stuck.

Surface Items that are poly-bagged, poly-wrapped, or otherwise covered in plastic make it hard for the postal service to print barcodes for optimal scanning. Certain types of coated papers can also be problematic in this regard.

Color and Pattern Paper stocks that are patterned or that contain dark fibers can interfere with processing, as the flecks or patterns can be mistaken by computer scanners as part of the address or barcode information.

Closures Envelopes that forego glued or taped seal flaps in favor of clasps, strings, buttons, or other dimensional embellishments may jam equipment.

United States Postal Service guidelines also specify addressing requirements, including acceptable use of halftone screens, correct placement of address windows or labels, and even preferred typographic styles and character spacing for address information. For the most current standards, visit the U.S. Postal Service website at www.usps.com and download the latest *Domestic Mail Manual* (DMM). For postal regulations outside of the United States, visit the websites on pages 25 and 26 for the most up-to-date information.

With a little creativity, you can print just one side of a press sheet and have artwork on both the front and back of an envelope once the envelope is converted. You can even bring the art straight up to the fold line if you desire.

COUNTRY	USA
DESIGN FIRM	Belyea
CREATIVE DIRECTOR	Patricia Belyea
DESIGNER	Ben Reynolds
CLIENT	Belyea
PRINTER	ColorGraphics

POSTAGE DO

Will your clever envelope pass muster with your postal system? Failing to find out ahead of time could be a major blunder. You don't want to discover that your envelopes are nondeliverable after they've been printed, stuffed, and dropped in the mail. Before you start production, share your concept with your local post office and ask for feedback. Fax a description that spells out all the project specs (including size, ink colors, ink coverage, paper stock, etc) and ask for comments and a signature of approval.

INTERNATIONAL POSTAL SERVICE WEBSITES

ÅLAND	Åland Post	www.posten.aland.fi/start.con
ARGENTINA	Correo Argentino	www.correoargentino.com.ar
ASCENSION ISLAND	Ascension Island Post Office and Philatelic Bureau	www.postoffice.gov.ac
AUSTRALIA	Australia Post	www.auspost.com.au
AUSTRIA	Austrian Poastal Services—PTA-Post and Telekom Austria	www.pta.at
BELGIUM	De Post—La Poste—Die Post	www.post.be
BERMUDA	Bermuda General Post Office	www.bermudapostoffice.com
BRAZIL	Correios (Postal Administration of Brazil)	www.correios.com.br
BRUNEI DARUSSALAM	Brunei Postal Services Department	www.post.gov.bn
BULGARIA	Bulgarian Posts	www.bgpost.bg
CAMBODIA	Ministry of Posts	www.mptc.gov.kh
CANADA	Canada Post/Postes Canada	www.canadapost.ca
CHANNEL ISLANDS	Guernsey Post Limited	www.guernseypost.com
CHILE	Correos de Chile	www.correos.cl
CHINA	China Post	www.chinapost.gov.cn/english
COSTA RICA	Correos de Costa Rica	www.correos.go.cr/correoswebsite_ingles/index_in.php
CROATIA	Hvratska Posta	www.posta.hr
CZECH REPUBLIC	Ceska Posta	www.cpost.cz
DENMARK	Post Danmark	www.postdanmark.dk
ESTONIA	Eesti Post	www.post.ee
FAROE ISLANDS	Postverk Føroya	www.stamps.fo
FIJI	Post Fiji	www.postfiji.com.fj
FINLAND	Suomen Posti Oy	www.posti.fi
FRANCE	La Poste Française	www.laposte.fr
FRENCH POLYNESIA	Philatelic Center	www.tahiti-postoffice.com
GERMANY	Deutsche Post	www.deutschepost.de/postagen
GREECE	Hellenic Post	www.elta-net.gr
HONDURAS	Correos de Honduras	www.honduras.net/honducor/index.html
HONG KONG	Hongkong Post	www.hongkongpost.com
HUNGARY	Posta	www.posta.hu

INTERNATIONAL POSTAL SERVICE WEBSITES *continued*

ICELAND	Iceland Post	www.postur.is/haht/vefur
IRELAND	An Post	www.anpost.ie
ISLE OF MAN POST	Isle of Man Post	www.iompostoffice.com
JAMAICA	Postal Corporation of Jamaica Ltd	www.jamaicapost.gov.jm
JAPAN	Postal Services Agency	www.yusei.go.jp/eng/english/english-index.html
JORDAN	Jordan Ministry of Post and Communications	www.jordanpost.com.jo
KAZAKHSTAN	Kazpost	www.kazpost.kz
LATVIA	Latvijas Posts/Latvia Post	www.post.lv
LESOTHO	Lesotho Postal Services	www.lps.org.ls
LITHUANIA	Lithuania Post	www.post.lt
LUXEMBOURG	P and T Luxembourg—Postes	www.postes.lu
MAURITIUS	Ministry of Information Technology and Telecommunications—Postal Services Division	ncb.intnet.mu/mitt/postal/index.htm
NETHERLANDS ANTILLES	Post Netherlands Antilles	www.postna.com
NEW ZEALAND	New Zealand Post	www.nzpost.co.nz
NICARAGUA	Correos de Nicaragua	www.correos.com.ni
NORWAY	Posten	www.posten.no
PAKISTAN	Pakistan Post	www.pakpost.gov.pk
PHILIPPINES	Philippine Postal Corporation	www.philpost.gov.ph
PITCAIRN ISLAND	Pitcairn Island Mail and Stamps	www.lareau.org//pitmail.html
POLAND	Poczta Polska	www.poczta-polska.pl
PORTUGAL	Correios de Portugal	www.ctt.pt
POSTAL CORPORATION OF KENYA	Posta Kenya	www.posta.co.ke
REPUBLIC OF CYPRUS	Cyprus Postal Services	www.pio.gov.cy
REPUBLIC OF MALDIVES	Maldives Post Ltd	www.maldivespost.com
SAINT HELENA	The Island of St. Helena Post Office and Philatelic Bureau	www.postoffice.gov.sh
SINGAPORE	Singapore Post	www.singpost.com.sg
SLOVAKIA	Slovenska Posta	www.slposta.sk
SOUTH AFRICA	South African Post Office	www.sapo.co.za
SWEDEN	Sweden Post	www.posten.se
SWITZERLAND	La Poste—La Posta—Die Post	www.post.ch
TANZANIA	Tanzania Posts Corporation	www.tanpost.com
THAILAND	Communications Authority of Thailand	www.cat.or.th
UKRAINE	Ukrainian Post Home Page	www.ukrposhta.com
UNITED KINGDOM	Royal Mail	www.royalmail.co.uk
	British Forces Post Office	www.bfpo.org.uk
	Royal Mail *Includes a finder for post codes and post office.*	www.royalmail.com
	Post Office Reform *News and information on the changes being brought about in the postal market*	www.dti.gov.uk/postalservices/network.htm

Window Envelopes

Window envelopes can be ideal for large direct mail campaigns because they eliminate the need to laser and synchronize addresses on both inserts and envelopes. If you are creating a window envelope for a mass mailing, chances are your mail piece will need to qualify for automated processing. Make sure your design specifications meet postal regulations before your envelopes go into production.

There are several kinds of translucent materials that can be used for the window pane, including poly, cello, and glassine. The optimal material may be determined by the glue you are using or by postal requirements. It's best to discuss your needs with your printer or envelope converter in advance so they can specify the best choice.

Window positions are measured from the left side and bottom of the envelope, with the flap at the top. Check with your converter or post office to make sure your envelope design meets the minimum clearance requirements for window placement.

Horizontal Windows

Vertical Windows

Customizing Premade Envelopes

If you prefer not to convert envelopes from scratch, you can always customize premade envelopes that you buy off the shelf. Graphics can be printed on stock envelopes that have already been converted.

If your job will be printed on a standard lithographic press, keep in mind you'll need to leave a ¼" (0.6 cm), nonprinted margin along the top and left side of the envelope to accommodate the guide mechanisms that feed the paper through the press. You can avoid this requirement by printing your job on a jet printer. The new jet printers do a respectable job with art that bleeds. They can also print spot graphics on both sides of the envelope in one press pass, provided there is minimal ink coverage on each side.

Printing isn't the only way to customize a standard envelope. Foil stamping, stickers, and other embellishments can also add unique flair.

Working with Printers and Converters

Occasionally, you will find a vendor that offers both printing and converting, but usually printers subcontract envelope assembly to specialty converters. A conversion house will have all the necessary equipment to cut,

IMPERIAL ENVELOPE STYLES

Announcement

A2	4³/₈ X 5³/₄	**A8**	5¹/₂ X 8¹/₈
A6	4³/₄ X 6¹/₂	**A10**	6 X 9¹/₂
A7	5¹/₄ X 7¹/₄	**Slimline**	3⁷/₈ X 8⁷/₈

Side seam design used for invitations, greeting cards, or small booklets.

Baronial

4½	3⁵/₈ X 5¹/₈	**6**	4³/₄ X 6¹/₂
5	4¹/₈ X 5¹/₂	**Lee**	5¹/₄ X 7¹/₄
5½	4³/₈ X 5³/₄	**8**	5³/₄ X 8

Diagonal seam design used for invitations and announcements.

Booklet

5¹/₂ X 7¹/₂	9 X 12
6 X 9	10 X 13
7 X 10	

Side seam featuring a wallet flap along the longer side. Booklet envelopes are sometimes referred to by mail fulfillment houses as open side envelopes.

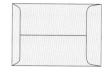

Catalog

5¹/₂ X 7¹/₂	9 X 12
6 X 9	10 X 13
7 X 10	

Center seam with wallet flap along the shorter side. Often used for mailing and shipping in large quantities. Referred to by fulfillment houses as open end.

Commercial Diagonal Flap

Check	3⁵/₈ X 8⁵/₈	**No.10½**	4¹/₂ X 9¹/₂
No.9	3⁷/₈ X 8⁷/₈	**No.11**	4¹/₂ X 10³/₈
No.10	4¹/₈ X 9¹/₂	**No.12**	4³/₄ X 11

Side seam design used for invitations, greeting cards, or small booklets.

Commercial Square Flap

No.10	4¹/₈ X 9¹/₂

score, fold, and glue envelopes in a range of sizes and styles. Note that an envelope converter is not the same thing as a mail house. (A mail house handles database management, imprinting of addresses, stuffing, sealing, and mailing after the manufacturing process is complete.)

Even if you're a hands-on kind of designer, you're best off relying on your printer to manage the job at the envelope converter. Maintaining a single point of contact for your project from start to finish can be very beneficial—namely because if anything goes wrong during the conversion stage, the printer will negotiate on your behalf to fix the problem. Also, converters typically reserve specific days of the week to run certain styles of envelopes. The printer will be familiar with this schedule and may be able to achieve priority status for your job, moving it up in the queue.

A QUESTION OF QUANTITY

For custom jobs, you can order as small a number of envelopes as you like, but generally you will be paying a printer or conversion house for a minimum run of 1,000. For large orders, you may find that printing and converting the envelopes you've designed is actually less expensive than buying preconverted envelopes.

IMPERIAL ENVELOPE STYLES

Monarch

$3^7/_8$ X $7^1/_2$

Diagonal or side seam design, traditionally used for personal correspondence.

Policy

No. 10½	$4^1/_2$ X $9^1/_2$
No. 11	$4^1/_2$ X $10^3/_8$

Center seam with end flap on the short end. Historically used to hold insurance policies (hence the name), this style has been recently resurrected for alternative uses.

Square

5½	$5^1/_2$ X $5^1/_2$	**7**	7 X 7
6	6 X 6	**7½**	$7^1/_2$ X $7^1/_2$
6½	$6^1/_2$ X $6^1/_2$	**8**	8 X 8

Used for unique items such as invitations, announcements, and odd-sized booklets. Most often features side seam construction. Note: square envelopes incur a postage surcharge in the U.S.

ISO (INTERNATIONAL) ENVELOPE STYLES

Announcement

C6	114 X 162 mm
C7/8	81 X 162 mm

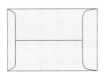

Catalog

CO	917 X 1297 mm	**C3**	324 X 458 mm
C1	648 X 917 mm	**C4**	229 X 324 mm
C2	458 X 648 mm	**C5**	162 X 229 mm

Commercial

DL	110 X 220 mm

Troubleshooting with Mail Houses

If your envelopes will be mailed, be sure to contact your mail house (if you plan to use one) during the design phase to communicate your fulfillment needs up front. Will your job need to qualify for automated insertion? If you're looking to mail 10,000 pieces, for example, manual stuffing may be prohibitively expensive. In this case, you'll want to design an envelope that can be machine stuffed. The inserting machine at the mail house may only be able to accommodate certain envelope dimensions, flap styles, and flap lengths. It will also require a certain amount of clearance between the envelope body and flap so the inserts slide in easily.

Addressing issues should also be discussed in advance with the mail house. You'll want to avoid varnishes and coatings on the area of the envelope that will be addressed. Test your addressing method—whether it involves imprinting or labeling—during the design phase. If the mail house is unfamiliar with your paper stock, send a sample for pretesting. If there are problems with the stock, you may need to change your paper specifications or addressing method.

Common Pitfalls

Most envelope nightmares can be avoided with forethought, planning, and solid communication between designer, printer, converter, and mail house. Here are some common conundrums and how to avoid them.

Poor Fit Obviously an envelope that is too small for its contents is a problem. Conversely, an envelope that is too large will look sloppy and unsophisticated. Always test your contents in their intended envelope beforehand. If the envelope is being converted, create a paper dummy for testing.

Graphics That Don't Line Up Accurate crossovers are hard to achieve when printing on diagonal seam envelopes. If the back of your envelope features a complex graphic, consider manufacturing a side-seam envelope instead.

Curling Seal Flaps It may be tempting to cut costs by specifying a lighter weight paper stock. However, an envelope with a full ink bleed printed on 60 lb. (27 kg) text weight or cheap stock may end up with a curled seal flap. This can make auto insertion troublesome and costly.

Cracking Specifying a paper stock that is too bulky (too heavy to fold and convert) can also be problematic. Heavier papers may need to be scored first so they don't crack once they are folded on a converting machine. A 65 lb. (29.5 kg) or 80 lb. (36 kg) cover weight sheet might be the heaviest that your converter can handle. Be sure to check first before you order paper.

Mailing Problems The majority of envelope problems occur after the envelopes are mailed. Before you send your job to the printer and converter, make sure your design complies with all relevant postal regulations and that the postage matches the weight of the package

---

SHOPPING FOR THE RIGHT PARTNER

Good communication with all vendor partners will make your envelope project run smoother. Here are some helpful questions to ask your printer and/or converter:

> Does the printer offer envelope conversion in-house? If not, where will the work be subcontracted? Ask to see samples of other envelope projects they've managed or executed.

> Can your envelopes be ganged up in multiples on a press sheet to save money and paper? Can the layout be reconfigured to fit more envelopes on a single sheet?

> Does your printer want to die-cut your blanks in-house before sending them out for conversion? Although this step adds cost to a project, it's a good idea for envelopes with critical color breaks on folds.

> Can the printer set up a tour of the converter's facility for you? Seeing the manufacturing process first-hand will give you a better understanding of how your design translates into a finished envelope.

and the speed of its delivery. If you are using an indicia, check that the correct account number appears on the envelope.

Storage Proper storage of envelopes is important to prevent the flaps from curling or sealing prematurely. Envelopes with remoistenable glue need to be stored in a dry place. If envelopes will be stored for a long time, seal the cartons and stack them with samples taped to the side of each box so it is clear what each box contains.

COUNTRY	USA
DESIGN FIRM	Belyea
CREATIVE DIRECTOR	Patricia Belyea
DESIGNER	Naomi Murphy
CLIENT	ColorGraphics
PRINTER	ColorGraphics

Graphics that wrap around an envelope from front to back may not align once the envelope is converted. Sometimes this can work to your advantage and create an interesting visual effect.

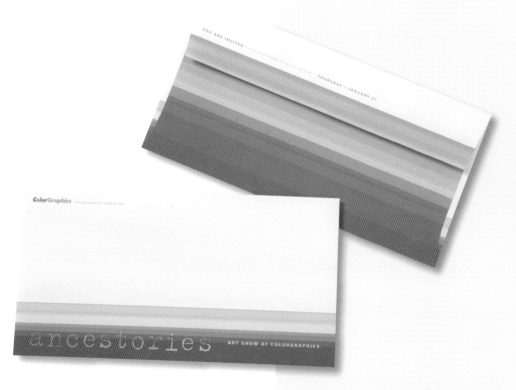

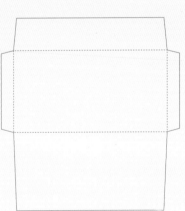

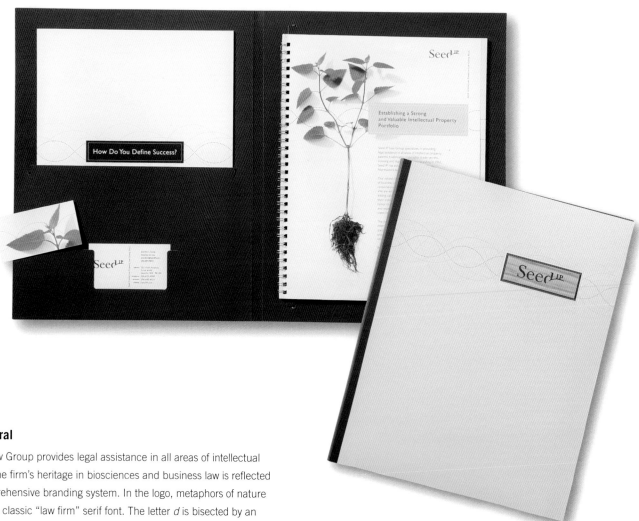

Look Natural

Seed IP Law Group provides legal assistance in all areas of intellectual property. The firm's heritage in biosciences and business law is reflected in its comprehensive branding system. In the logo, metaphors of nature meld with a classic "law firm" serif font. The letter *d* is bisected by an upward-arching horizon, invoking Seed clients' future-oriented quest for new ideas and groundbreaking inventions.

References to the natural world continue to delight in an extendable kit of parts. On the cover, a delicate scientific helix wends its way across a wooden placard that is letterpress printed with the Seed logo. The wood veneer tip-on is one of many production details that required special care; the letterpress craftsman had to mix ink on press to match Seed's standard PMS color. Multiple faux wood grains were considered, taking into account the toll that humidity and temperature might take in the long run.

The capacity folder cover, a super-thick, uncoated stock, is lined on the inside with a sheet of fiery orange (the firm's trademark accent color) for a custom duplex effect. Die-cut slots and tabs, created to hold materials of varying weights and sizes, make interesting shapes. And the crowning detail, a business card inserted into the inside folder pocket, creates a relief shape resembling a flowerpot.

COUNTRY	USA
DESIGN FIRM	Hornall Anderson Design Works
CREATIVE DIRECTORS	Jack Anderson & Kathy Saito
DESIGNERS	Jack Anderson, Kathy Saito, & Henry Yiu
CLIENT	Seed IP Law Group
PRINTER	Evergreen Quality Press

Jennifer L. Scully
Attorney at Law
jennifers@SeedIP.com
206.694.4855

address 701 Fifth Avenue
Suite 6300
Seattle, WA 98104
telephone 206.622.4900
facsimile 206.682.6031
website SeedIP.com

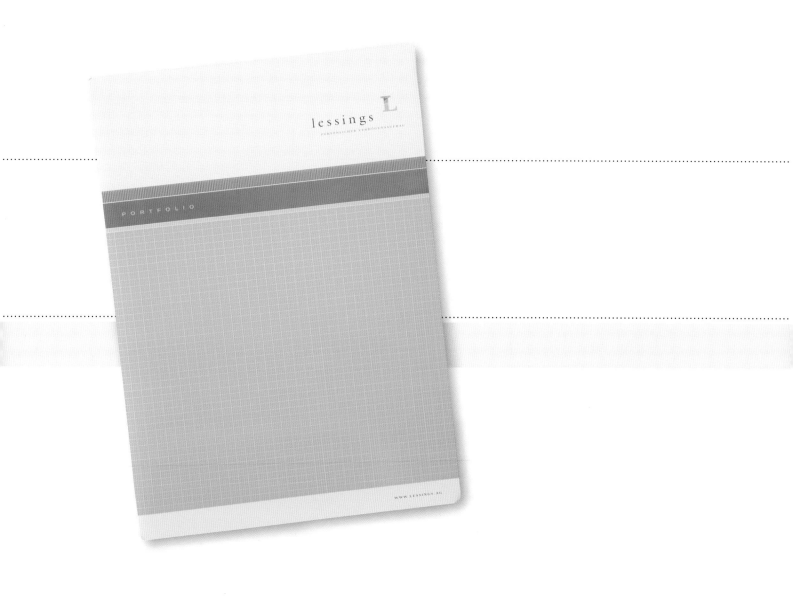

Smart Investment

Lessings is a small, independent financial consultancy geared toward students and young academics. The firm needed a marketing portfolio that would convey a sense of security and stability, but at the same time appeal to the revolutionary aesthetic sensibilities of younger generations.

Designers at Simon & Goetz meted their production dollars shrewdly. The folder's vivid palette of lime green, lemon yellow, and cerulean blue is a bold differentiator from the competition. To achieve this effect, multiple proofs were created on different paper stocks to test ink fidelity.

The folder is also distinguished by unusual textures and optics. Raised type and dimensional grids were achieved with an experimental UV lacquer process. An embossed logo in the upper-left corner complements this tactile, high-gloss surface. Radius corners are echoed in the rounded tabs of the business card slot. Tab flaps folding inward from the top and bottom hold paper inserts in place when the folder is closed.

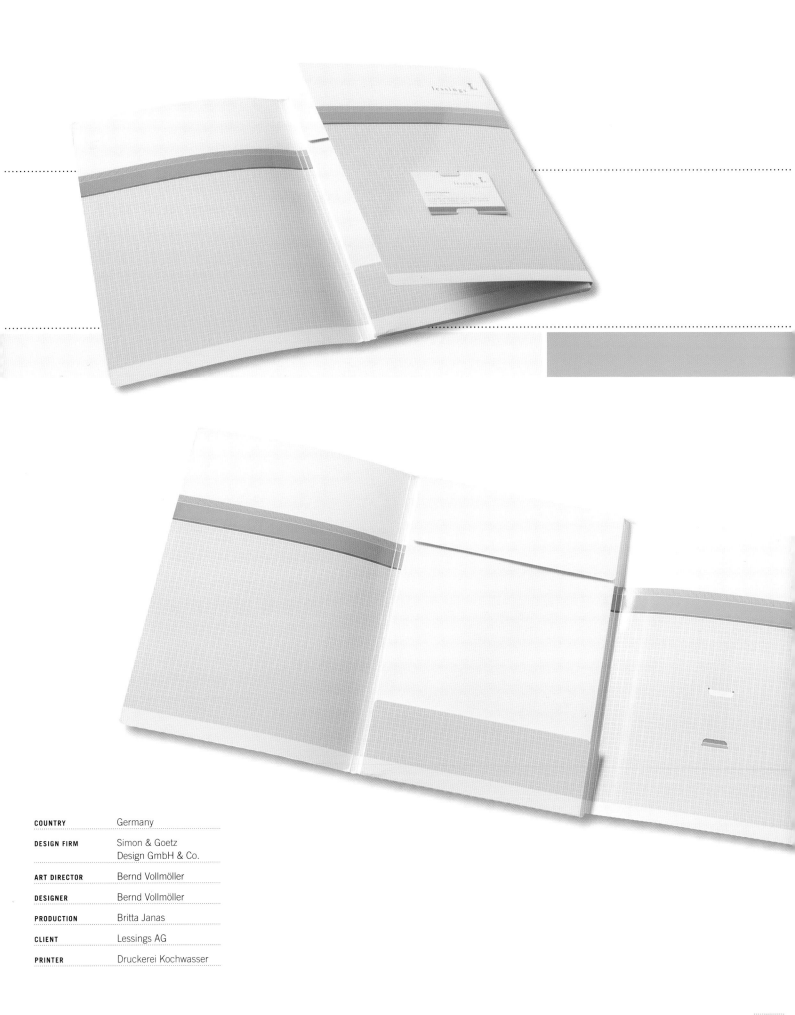

COUNTRY	Germany
DESIGN FIRM	Simon & Goetz Design GmbH & Co.
ART DIRECTOR	Bernd Vollmöller
DESIGNER	Bernd Vollmöller
PRODUCTION	Britta Janas
CLIENT	Lessings AG
PRINTER	Druckerei Kochwasser

Positive Vibes

Originally hired to rebrand radio station Z95.3 in Vancouver, **dossier**creative was soon asked to design a dual-purpose folder that could be used by both Z95.3 and one of its sister stations, CISL. The solution? A striking, customizable cover, made possible by a wraparound sticker label that nests inside a debossed plane.

Initially, the cover's logo-inspired dot pattern—a riff on graphic equalizer sound waves—was specified as a deboss as well. The design team later opted to render this motif with a combination of matte and gloss varnishes. Petite notches on the outside edges of the folder guide the angled elastic band into the correct position.

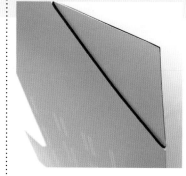

COUNTRY	Canada
DESIGN FIRM	**dossier**creative inc.
CREATIVE DIRECTOR	Don Chisholm
DESIGNER	Patrick Smith
CLIENT	Standard Radio (Z95.3 and CISL)
PRINTER	Lulu Island Printers

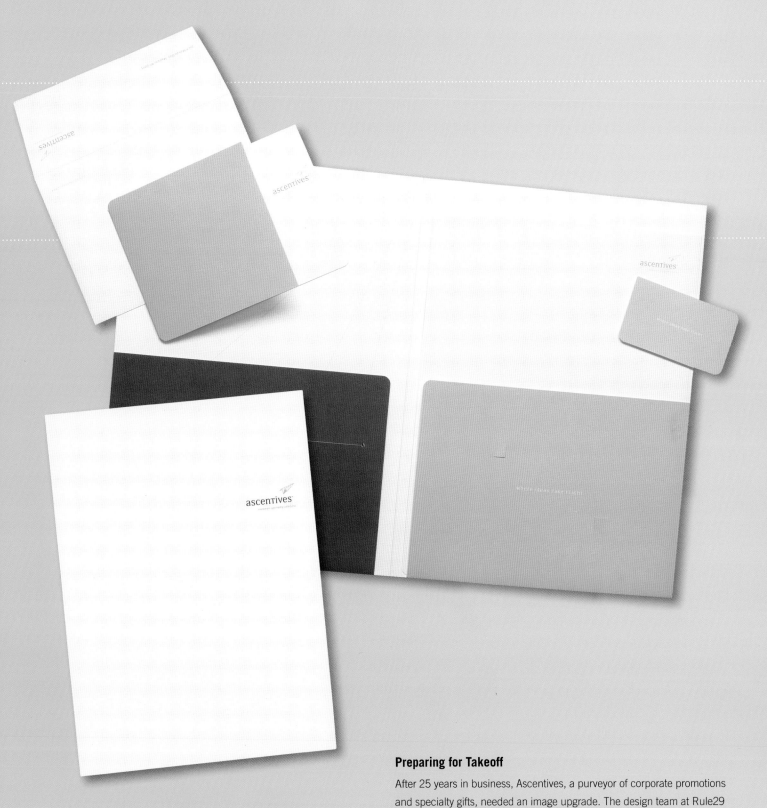

COUNTRY	USA
DESIGN FIRM	Rule29
CREATIVE DIRECTOR	Justin Ahrens
DESIGNERS	Justin Ahrens & Jim Boborci
CLIENT	Ascentives
PRINTER	O'Neil Printing

Preparing for Takeoff

After 25 years in business, Ascentives, a purveyor of corporate promotions and specialty gifts, needed an image upgrade. The design team at Rule29 gave the company's longstanding paper airplane icon a tune-up and then parlayed the logo's aerodynamic lines into a suite of collateral pieces underscoring the tagline, "Helping Your Ideas Take Flight."

The presentation folder is clean and modern on the outside and continues to engage on the inside. Tongue-in-cheek paper airplane fold lines radiate from the gutter, and clever die-cuts recast business cards as interesting shapes. Deep-capacity pockets and radius corners complete the package.

Menu of Services

When your target audience includes ink junkies and printophiles, you don't have to worry about speaking in lay terms. A spicy promo kit for The Production Kitchen, a print production company, converses in the vernacular of the printing business. All of its elements refer to the print production vocabulary, including a system of icons and patterns drawn from everyday artifacts found in prepress shops and on the pressroom floor.

The repeat pattern on the kit folder is derived from a printer's registration marks. The envelope is made to resemble a job jacket. And then there's that unmistakable neon orange block type that usually signifies proofs. For added flavor, Bløk Design varnished the type to make it pop. The capacity folder features an oversized flap with a die-cut tab closure.

COUNTRY	Canada
DESIGN FIRM	Bløk Design
CREATIVE DIRECTOR	Vanessa Eckstein
DESIGNER	Vanessa Eckstein
CLIENT	The Production Kitchen
PRINTER	Sommerset Graphics

COUNTRIES	USA/Chile
DESIGN FIRM	Templin Brink
CREATIVE DIRECTORS	Joel Templin & Gaby Brink
DESIGNER	Paul Howalt
ILLUSTRATOR	Michael Schwab
CLIENT	Robert Modavi
PRINTER	Art Real

A Good Vintage

Sales kits for vintners are usually glossy packages laden with photos of staged culinary spreads. The sales folder for Caliterra, a wine partnership between the Mondavi family of Napa and the Chadwick family of Chile, takes an alternate route. A rich, stylized cover illustration evokes the romanticism of old travel posters.

Inside, the folder is printed the hue of antique parchment and reads like a travel log, featuring postcards, stickers, a "passport to Chile," and facts about Chile's wine region. A three-hole-punched lip on the side of the piece allows it to be inserted in a binder.

Digital by Design

The Microsoft Visio "experience tour" provides Microsoft's sales force with an innovative tool for presenting Visio as an enterprise-level business solution to corporate decision-makers. For this sophisticated audience, the digital demo had to be sharp, smart, and attention grabbing. The project's primary design metaphor (as seen on the folder cover) is Visio's well-known diagramming style, which is used for the navigation of the demo, and as a visual element in print.

The digital design was the cool "money item" that drove most of the creative in the supporting collateral. A centered, foam-dot clasp on the inside folder pocket allows the CD-ROM to play a starring role in the layout. Matte UV coating gives the durable folder a smooth, high-tech texture.

COUNTRY	USA
DESIGN FIRM	Methodologie
CREATIVE DIRECTOR	Minh Nguyen
DESIGNER	Minh Nguyen
CLIENT	Microsoft
PRINTER	ColorGraphics

Artful Structure

Leers Weinzapfel is a Boston-based architectural firm known for its socially conscious commissions. Its versatile capabilities folder needed to reflect the firm's allegiance to conceptual clarity, aesthetic balance, and material integrity, as well as its predilection for spare forms.

Engineering proved critical to the success of this unique folder. A super-weight cardstock, custom manufactured using special paper processing methods, was die-cut with subtle radius corners. The unique metal snap closure (which alleviates the need for glue) required several rounds of experiments in the best hole-punching method to adhere metal to cardstock.

The final folder is a savory expression of the firm's modernist ideals. On the cover, a shiny square label and circular black metal snap contrast the toothy surface of the metallic cardboard. The folder itself becomes an architectural object that commands attention, while complementing the materials inside.

COUNTRY	USA
DESIGN FIRM	Nassar Design
CREATIVE DIRECTOR	Nelida Nassar
DESIGNERS	Nelida Nassar & Margarita Encomienda
COPYWRITER	Gabrielle Angevine
PHOTOGRAPHER	Nassar Design
CLIENT	Leers Weinzapfel Architects
PRINTER	Alpha Press

Better Half

Designers at Noon desired an all-purpose folder to house proposals, letters, business cards, tear sheets, and press releases in an organized, yet stylish, manner. The folder needed to complement the studio's letterhead system, yet remain neutral so as not to clash with potentially colorful inserts.

After failing to find an unflecked cardstock in the right hue, the team tried making a custom duplex stock by backing up two lighter weight sheets, but this option was pricey and the results looked sloppy. A more cost-effec-

tive solution was to print an inexpensive cardstock with two hits of custom brown ink, thereby achieving the desired color and weight.

The folder's revealing format is both interesting and economical in its paper use. A foreshortened cover allows the contents to serve as part of the face presentation. For flexible flair, the color of the ribbon closure varies, depending on the contents of each piece.

COUNTRY	USA
DESIGN FIRM	Noon
CREATIVE DIRECTOR	Cinthia Wen
DESIGNERS	Tomo Ito & Cinthia Wen
CLIENT	Noon
PRINTER	Oscar Printing
PRINT CONSULTANT	Frank La

Tall, Stark, and Handsome

Located in downtown Seattle, the Bank of America Tower is one of the tallest buildings on the West Coast. Working with Wright Runstad and Equity Office, Methodologie developed new positioning and marketing materials to attract upscale tenants following a significant building renovation.

A sophisticated, leasing brochure kit presents the tower as "The Vertical City" where one can dine, work, and shop in one place. The folder itself is unusually tall and slim, accentuated by an elegant, decorative die-cut slot in the cover. Inside, this verticality is further emphasized by dramatic black-and-white photography. The back pocket is constructed of a flap that folds from the right and glues along the top and bottom edges. A die-cut in the flap creates a slot for inserts.

COUNTRY	USA
DESIGN FIRM	Methodologie
CREATIVE DIRECTOR	Ann Traver
DESIGNER	Leo Raymundo
PHOTOGRAPHER	Remy Haynes
CLIENT	Equity Office/ Wright Runstad
PRINTER	Rainier Color

Building Blocks

When the Quadrant, a 12,000-sq.-meter commercial property in central Amsterdam, was vacated, the realtor needed a savory marketing piece to woo prospective renters. Although the goal was to lease the whole building to a single tenant, the realtor realized it might have to split the property. A hybrid brochure-folder was created to hold individual floor plans should the property need to be divided and leased in parts.

The folder's strong, geometric construction evokes the architecture of the building itself. Three die-cut windows frame the site's main selling points (central location, proximity to public transportation, and good internal facilities). A metallic blue ink evokes the tone of the building façade and a spot gloss varnish adds dimension to typographic passages. Several hand dummies were created to make sure the die-cut windows fell in the correct place before the job went to the finisher.

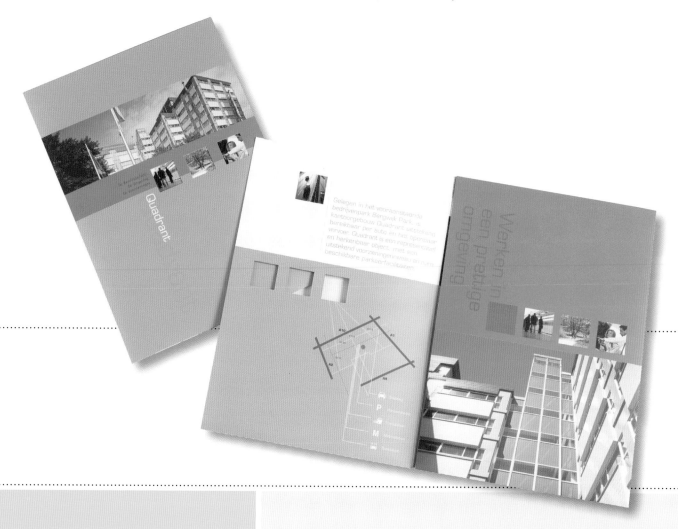

COUNTRIES	Israel/Netherlands
DESIGN FIRM	Jason & Jason Visual Communication
CREATIVE DIRECTOR	Jonathan Jason
ART DIRECTOR /DESIGNER	Tamar Lourie
COPYWRITER	Mila van Geesink, TradukoenCommunicatie
CLIENT	CB Richard Ellis
PRINTER	Yahalomi Zisman

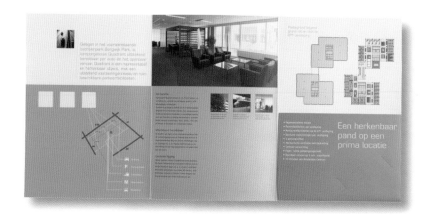

COUNTRY	UK
DESIGN FIRM	Blue River Design Ltd.
SENIOR DESIGNER	Lisa Thundercliffe
ACCOUNT MANAGER	Jane Longrigg
CLIENT	Waygood Centre for Artists
PRINTERS	HFW Plastics, Field Print, Bryson Print, & Billingham Press

A Clear Solution

Waygood is a thriving contemporary arts center in the city of Newcastle, offering artist studios, a gallery space, and artist-led contemporary arts education. Founded in the first floor of a vacant warehouse, Waygood hoped to raise £5.07 million to expand and occupy the entire six-story building. Its fund-raising package needed to be orthodox enough to appeal to serious corporate patrons without downplaying the creative experimentation for which the center was known.

Designers at Blue River investigated a range of folder styles that could be customized to hold a CD, an A4 business plan, a small brochure, and a business card. A transparent plastic ultimately allowed the literature inside the folder to add "color and life" to the pitch (a nice metaphor for the energy generated by the artists inside the building).

Several plastics were considered. Designers wanted a substrate that would contrast nicely with the matte finish of the printed inserts as well as the glossy stickers affixed to each collateral piece. Prototypes helped sell the design concept to the client and ensured the print literature would fit snugly inside the plastic pockets. Postage was not an issue, as folders were primarily distributed during face-to-face presentations.

COUNTRY	USA
DESIGN FIRM	Nassar Design
CREATIVE DIRECTOR	Nelida Nassar
DESIGNERS	Nelida Nassar & Margarita Encomienda
COPYWRITER	Nassar Design
PHOTOGRAPHER	Nassar Design
PRINTER	Creative Finishing Inc.

Fresh Sheets

Nassar Design's relocation to a new studio space presented an opportunity for an identity redesign. The creative team savored the excuse to experiment with a new line of vellum papers in luscious citrus colors (Cromatica by Thibierge & Comar). The folder housing the firm's promotional collateral had to complement this tart and tasty palette while holding its own. Nassar found its solution in tran-e-wave, a fanciful corrugated sheet (part of the Chatham Translucents line from Reich Papers) that is both translucent and opaque, as well as acid-free, recyclable, and biodegradable.

Because they are corrugated, the folders do not scuff and can be stacked and stored economically. The major drawback is that the textured surface cannot be printed on. A channel-scored, silk-screened sticker is affixed to each folder cover.

Corner Window

The multipurpose folder for Quiver, a provider of categorization, search-and-retrieval software, is all about high performance. Used as a shell for media kits, new business pitches and leave-behinds, the deep-capacity jacket serves as a quiver of sorts, holding information on a variety of tools and services (arrows) in the company arsenal.

Coated industrial board, offset printed with a spot varnish, lends durability to the piece. Embossing adds a touch of elegance to the cover's otherwise utilitarian aesthetic. The entire package is held closed by sturdy side tabs that wrap around a hinged end flap and lock into die-cut slits.

To create visual continuity among various insert materials, Templin Brink designed a clear vellum sleeve that can be earmarked with color-coded stickers or tabs. The stickers align behind a die-cut window that wraps around the corner of the folder box, offering a cross-section view of what's inside. The kit's colorful coding system and sheath format were inspired by the oversized jackets that hold radiology films.

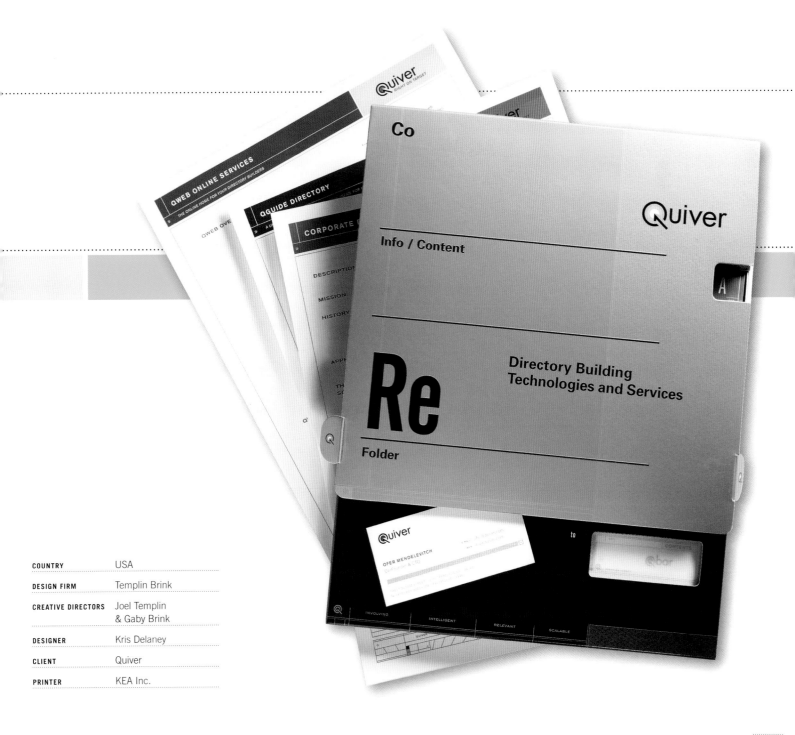

COUNTRY	USA
DESIGN FIRM	Templin Brink
CREATIVE DIRECTORS	Joel Templin & Gaby Brink
DESIGNER	Kris Delaney
CLIENT	Quiver
PRINTER	KEA Inc.

Chromatherapy

Fund-raising materials for a capital campaign supporting a new cancer center needed to feel weighty, but not funereal. The goal was to inspire corporations and individual philanthropists to invest with optimism.

A vibrant capacity sleeve of colorful squares evokes the language of digital medical technology, as well as the colors of various cancer ribbons. To avoid an unfinished look on the blank inside of the slipcover, designers at Bluelounge extended the trim size of the cover wrap to include 2" (5 cm) "tongues" that roll around the edges. The result is a cleaner case with a sturdier construction.

The vibrant palette is also applied to a matching presentation folder, in which ribbon colors are used as full-bleed section dividers representing specific types of cancer. Curved pocket folders give the piece a friendly countenance. The entire book was printed in CMYK, with photos rendered as poignant duotones. Image fidelity was important, but it was also critical that the piece not appear overly slick. A matte coated stock with a satin aqueous finish created just the right touch.

COUNTRY	USA
DESIGN FIRM	Bluelounge Design
CREATIVE DIRECTOR	Melissa Sunjaya
DESIGNERS	Melissa Sunjaya, Diana Sopha, & Hannae Kang
PHOTOGRAPHER	Steven Heller
COPYWRITER	Kelly Smith
COPY EDITOR	Stuart Frolick
CLIENT	Providence Saint Joseph
PRINTER	Graphic Visions Inc.

Blinding Commitment

Maiow Creative Branding craved a credentials piece that could be customized for individual prospects. The team designed and printed a set of interchangeable case study inserts that slips inside a pristine white folder. This substantial outer shell, printed sparely with the studio's name and a few tiny promises (for those inclined to read the small print), features multiple scores that can be activated to accommodate contents of varying girths.

The solution for collating each one-of-a-kind catalog is where things get especially interesting. Maiow spent part of its promo budget on an industrial sewing machine so it could stitch bind individual pieces in-house, using turquoise thread to match the cover type. Selecting paper stocks that wouldn't mangle a sewing needle was a key priority.

Inserts of varying page length—including a short-lipped intro page—create an immediate sense of discovery and intrigue inside each custom promo. The case studies are French folded, each with an illustrative poster side that unfolds to reveal project details. The handmade, bespoke quality of the finished article reflects the design firm's commitment to the total package, as well as the fine details.

COUNTRY	UK
DESIGN FIRM	Maiow Creative Branding
CREATIVE DIRECTOR	Paul Rapacioli
DESIGNERS	Steve Johnson, Ceri Lewis, & Dave Worthington
CLIENT	Maiow Creative Branding
PRINTER	Wood Mitchell

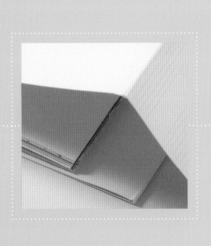

Good Shape

Gilon, an Israeli software developer, was pleased to form a strategic alliance with the consulting giant Deloitte & Touche. Suddenly, it needed a more sophisticated capabilities package that would open doors to international markets.

Its multipanel collateral folder makes a bold statement. Metallic inks juxtaposed with vibrant orange represent the confluence of business acumen and innovation. Unusual die-cuts on the cover convey the company's ability to supersede the status quo. The quadrangular window provides a unique view, and the angled wedge along the top edge allows Gilon's vibrant personality to shine through. The spine was designed with extra capacity to hold thick inserts.

COUNTRY	Israel
DESIGN FIRM	Jason & Jason Visual Communication
CREATIVE DIRECTOR	Jonathan Jason
ART DIRECTOR /DESIGNER	Dalia Inbar
CLIENT	Gilon - Deloitte & Touche
PRINTER	Yahalomi Zisman

Cause for Celebration

ESRA is a volunteer not-for-profit organization that provides assistance to new and underprivileged Israeli immigrants. A fund-raising package targeting corporate sponsors needed to appear polished and professional, but not indulgent.

Jason & Jason designed a functional and economical identity system with an uplifting palette and friendly typography. The two-color presentation folder, printed on uncoated stock, uses a tab-and-notch pocket closure in lieu of glue to minimize costs. Donations increased by 40 percent after the new identity system was introduced.

COUNTRY	Israel
DESIGN FIRM	Jason & Jason Visual Communication
CREATIVE DIRECTOR	Jonathan Jason
ART DIRECTOR /DESIGNER	Dalia Inbar
CLIENT	ESRA
PRINTER	A.R. Printing

COUNTRY	USA
DESIGN FIRM	Bluelounge Design
CREATIVE DIRECTOR	Melissa Sunjaya
DESIGNERS	Melissa Sunjaya & Diana Sopha
CLIENT	Skin Deep Laser Medspa
PRINTER	Graphic Visions Inc.

Second Skin

Engineering a brochure-folder for Skin Deep Laser Medspa involved starting at the end and working backward. Because the piece would travel by mail, a standard 9" X 12" (22.5 X 30 cm) folded trim size made sense to control postage costs. The question then became how to make a glowing impression within these dimensions while realizing economies on the production side. The size of the press sheet ultimately dictated the template design for a three-panel folder with one panel pocket.

A related challenge was that the folder pocket needed to house an assortment of inserts supplied by outside vendors, each sporting a different brand look and feel. To prevent a break in visual continuity, the pocket was generously sized to hide this potpourri of inserts underneath a cover letter.

Bluelounge had a choice between printing the folder two-up on the press sheet, or printing it one-up and using the extra real estate to run three additional postcards and six business cards. Because the specified folder quantity was small, the team went with the latter. This resulted in cost savings for the client's overall communications program.

BOMBARDIER
BUSINESS AIRCRAFT

COUNTRY	USA
DESIGN FIRM	Greteman Group
CREATIVE DIRECTOR	Sonia Greteman
DESIGNERS	James Strange & Marc Bosworth
CLIENT	Bombardier Aerospace
PRINTER	Printing Inc.

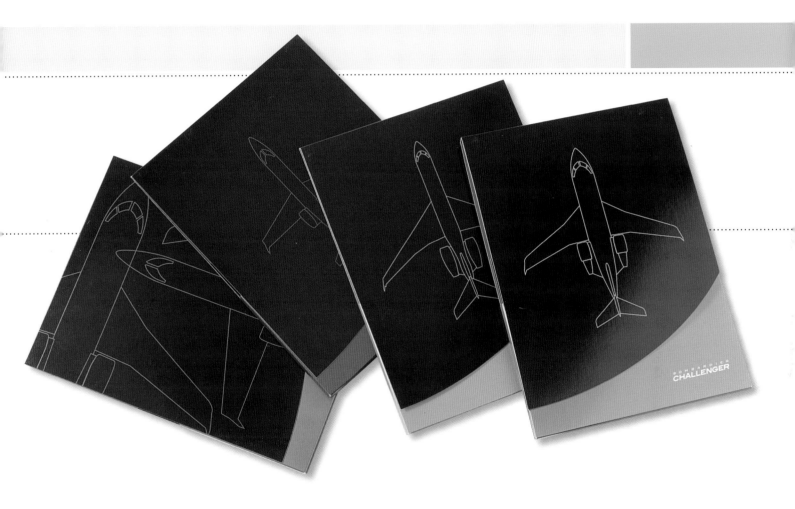

Perfect Landing

For the Paris Airshow during summer 2003, Bombardier Aerospace wanted a fleet of press kit folders that would soar above the rest. The sleek and memorable solution features four folder variations representing four planes in the Bombardier line. The metallic inks and arc-shaped folder flap are aerodynamic by design.

During the concept phase, Greteman Group presented a materials board to the client with various folding dummies constructed of actual paper samples. Preliminary directions explored foil stamping and embossing, as well as the possibility of a custom duplex stock. These specs were eventually scaled back to keep the cost per unit down, but luxury wasn't completely nixed from production. To achieve a rich, black sheen as deep as the night sky, ink densities were doubled using a dry-trap process. Note the matching CD case that nests inside the belly of the folder.

Being There

Nothing compares to being courtside at a Seattle Sonics game. But a recruitment package targeting potential season ticket holders (as well as standing ticket holders interested in upgrades) sought to come in a close second.

Designed to exude the excitement and energy of a live game experience, Hornall Anderson's folder delivers big time. Interesting juxtapositions of scale make for a dynamic cover. The folder's multipanel configuration creates a sense of anticipatory pacing as the piece unfolds. Brawny type, provocative copy, and full-bleed photos of players and fans team up for a full court press. And there's a prize inside: a perforated foldout poster of former Sonics forward guard, Desmond Mason.

The client was happy with the outcome, although midway through the season, the Sonics traded two of the players who appeared on the folder and sell sheets. Game over.

HE DEFINITELY DOESN'T HAVE A FEAR OF

FLYING

COUNTRY	USA
DESIGN FIRM	Hornall Anderson Design Works
CREATIVE DIRECTOR	Jack Anderson
DESIGNERS	Jack Anderson, Mark Popich, Andrew Wicklund, & Elmer dela Cruz
PHOTOGRAPHER	Jeff Reinking/ NBAE Photos
COPYWRITER	Ian Cohen
CLIENT	Seattle Sonics
PRINTER	ColorGraphics

Prairie Chic

Vintage cowboy never looked so debonair as in this promotional package for Lajitas, an upscale casual resort in the heart of Texas's Big Bend National Park. The resort logo seems branded (it's actually engraved) on handmade papers as rich and durable as tanned leather. The saddle-bag-style capacity folder features an oversized flap with a curved, die-cut enclosure.

Tiered inserts inside the folder showcase the full spectrum of resort amenities for an audience of event planners and travel professionals. Sepia-toned photographs in the matchbook-bound brochure and inserts complement the warm, rustic hues of the folder and envelope.

COUNTRY	USA
DESIGN FIRM	David Carter Design Associates
CREATIVE DIRECTOR	Ashley Barron Mattocks
DESIGNER	Donna Aldridge
COPYWRITER	1400 Words
PHOTOGRAPHER	Michael Wilson
MAP ILLUSTRATIONS	Elvis Swift
CLIENT	Lajitas
PRINTER	Williamson Printing Corp.
ENGRAVER/ DIE-CUTTING	Process Engraving

Folder in the Round

Simplicity reigns supreme in an experimental folder created for the Museum Documentation Center, an institution promoting museum activities in Croatia. Rectangular inserts are allowed to protrude from the folder's bowed edge, prompting a dialogue between a curve and a straight line.

In flat form, the folder template is a circle with a skinny wedge of pie missing at six o'clock. The sliced bottom of the sphere folds up to form pocket flaps. Double scores along the spine and the pocket seams create extra capacity for thick inserts. The pocket flaps are dutifully finished with radius corners to complete the curvilinear effect. The whole piece was engineered as a one-color job with a matte finish.

COUNTRY	Croatia
DESIGN FIRM	Studio International
CREATIVE DIRECTOR	Boris Ljubičič
DESIGNER	Boris Ljubičič
CLIENT	The Museum Documentation Center
PRINTER	Graphic Art

COUNTRY	Canada
DESIGN FIRM	Riordon Design
CREATIVE DIRECTOR	Dan Wheaton
DESIGNER	Alan Krpan
COPYWRITER	Alan Krpan
CLIENT	Definitive Sound
PRINTER	Contact Creative Services

Wide-Screen Format

In the competitive world of home theater systems, Definitive Sound needed a distinctive folder to complement its existing stationery—one that could act, in part, like a soft-sell brochure. With this objective in mind, Riordon Design proposed a horizontal folder format with accompanying insert materials to fit this unique orientation.

Rich, bold colors play a starring role in this versatile piece. Lifestyle images and blurred photo backgrounds sell ambiance without being product-specific. The generic imagery allows the folder to be used for a number of purposes, including custom proposals and collateral kits. Photos drawn from royalty-free archives (and then modified) kept costs in check.

On the Plus Side

Stanwell, a diversified Australian energy company, wished to share its performance achievements with stakeholders, contractors, joint venture partners, and commercial entities. A parallel goal was to sell the strengths of its businesses to potential investors. The positive news in the report is underscored by the design of its presentation folder.

The capacity folder is based on a metaphor of positive and negative energy attracting to create harmony and balance. The folder illustrates Stanwell's vision of "balanced growth" and "value adding" in black and white, providing a nice complement to the full-color brochure inside. In the brochure, plus and minus symbols form a dynamic grid that connects layered imagery from the company's coal, wind, hydro, and bioenergy power-generating facilities. The same grid is blind embossed on the folder cover, lending an elegant texture to the surface. A clever die-cut on the inside pocket uses negative space to suggest a plus sign. The capacity spine is printed with tiny, screened type that reads "Smarter, Greener, Stanwell."

COUNTRY	Australia
DESIGN FIRM	Minale Bryce Design Strategy
GRAPHIC DESIGN ASSOCIATE	Michail Kowal
DESIGNER	Natalie Hall
CLIENT	Stanwell Corporation Ltd.
PRINTER	Fine Print

Call It a Draw

Research showed that competitors of Dobson & Toncic, an insurance broker, were all using photography in their marketing materials. So Riordon Design proposed illustration for the company's trifold presentation folder. A soft, warm palette and whimsical imagery give the piece a human touch. It's the antithesis of sterile.

Balancing the budget for the brochure-folder hybrid was a juggling act. Custom illustrations were a splurge. To offset this cost, other line items were lowered by sticking with a house variety of coated paper and limiting ink specs to CMYK with an overall varnish. The center pocket is a score flap with no glue. Marketing inserts and a matching direct mail campaign were nested on the same press sheet to maintain visual continuity, maximize paper usage, and streamline costs.

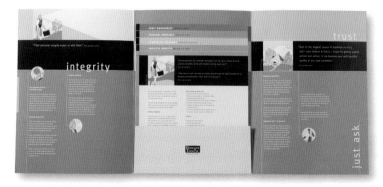

COUNTRY	Canada
DESIGN FIRM	Riordon Design
ART DIRECTOR	Ric Riordon
DESIGNERS	Dan Wheaton & Tim Warnock
COPYWRITER	Tim Turnbull
ILLUSTRATOR	Dan Wheaton
CLIENT	Dobson & Toncic
PRINTER	Contact Creative Services

Bountiful Crops

Ivara is a technology company specializing in asset reliability solutions. After building an identity system and website for the software-maker, Riordon Design was asked to create a presentation folder with a similar tech vibe.

Strong geometry and clean edges convey Ivara's allegiance to precision. The cropped-corner motif seen in various stationery pieces becomes three-dimensional in the folder's docked pocket. The corporate tagline is dry-trap printed on the folder cover with a clear spot varnish, creating an interesting visual dynamic between matte and gloss finishes. This solution allows the brand promise to shine through without overpowering the overall visual presentation.

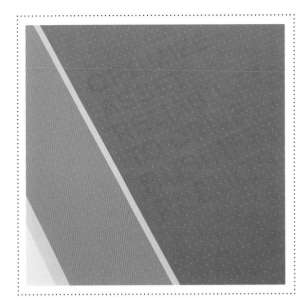

COUNTRY	Canada
DESIGN FIRM	Riordon Design
CREATIVE DIRECTOR	Dan Wheaton
DESIGNER	Alan Krpan
CLIENT	Ivara Corporation
PRINTER	Contact Creative Services

COUNTRY	Switzerland
DESIGN FIRM	superbüro
CREATIVE DIRECTOR	Barbara Ehrbar
DESIGNER	Barbara Ehrbar
CLIENT	Architektur Forum Biel

ARCHITEKTUR IN BIEL/
ARCHITECTURE À BIENNE

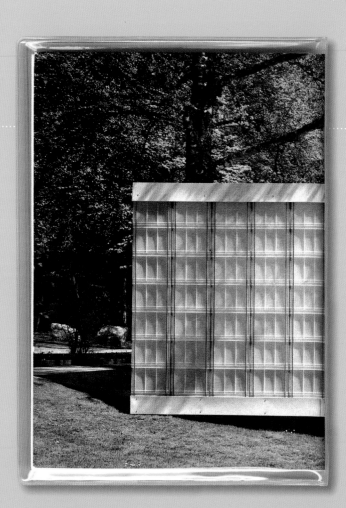

Pocket Full of Buildings

Architektur Forum Biel (The Architectural Guide to the City of Biel) was a prototype created for an awards program. An off-the-shelf A6 clear plastic folder holds a detailed map of the city. The folding map is accompanied by a companion booklet highlighting significant buildings and interiors in the landscape.

The translucent plastic folder protects its contents and gives the overall presentation a high gloss, while allowing the inserts to speak for themselves. The cover of the map becomes the cover of the folder; the back cover of the booklet becomes the back cover of the folder. As a result, the lightweight graphics on the front create an interesting tension when juxtaposed with the dense, colorful photography on back.

COUNTRY	Canada
DESIGN FIRM	Riordon Design
CREATIVE DIRECTOR	Dan Wheaton
DESIGNER	Amy Montgomery
CLIENT	x.eye inc.
PRINTER	Contact Creative Services

Eye-catching Design

x.eye inc. specializes in technology solutions that help banks, brokerages, insurers, and trusts increase assets under management. The fact that x.eye products and services are abstract, complex systems and not tangible things, posed a challenge for Riordon Design in conceiving a compelling, trifold brochure-folder. Loading the cover with trite imagery (such as dollar signs) or jargon wasn't the answer.

The design team ultimately focused on the company name as a metaphor. The x.eye logo peers through a die-cut peephole in the cover, enticing the viewer to turn the page. An interesting dual-textured folder stock adds to the intrigue. The cover bears a textured, linear finish, whereas the flip side is a smooth surface that's optimal for printing more detailed text, graphics, and images. Inside, the geometry of the design grid is complemented by unique, die-cut, business card slots. A flap along the bottom of the center panel folds up to create a small-capacity, nonglued pocket for letterhead.

Black Tie

British-born interior designer Susan Stockton is known for texturally decadent, upscale spaces. Her penchant for tactile luxuries is deftly captured in a chromatically spare capabilities folder that pulls out all the stops in the realm of touch. On the cover, a crisp, blind-embossed rendition of her trademark crown-and-bow logo perches above an engraving of the company name. A black satin ribbon is threaded through two holes and neatly tied. The black printed spine wraps to full black on the back of the folder, where the address is reversed to white.

Inside, a customizable vellum overlay highlighting the menu of services is layered on top of a white rendering of the firm's name, London by Design. The adjacent pocket features a custom sweeping shape (an echo of the folder's radius corners) and is printed in a deep violet to match the logo.

COUNTRY	USA
DESIGN FIRM	Becker Design
CREATIVE DIRECTOR	Neil Becker
DESIGNER	Neil Becker
CLIENT	London by Design
PRINTER	The Printery
ENGRAVER	Hart Engraving

COUNTRY	Australia
DESIGN FIRM	Flight Creative
ART DIRECTOR	Lisa Nankervis
DESIGNER	Lisa Nankervis
CLIENT	Ed Dixon Food Design
PRINTER	Bambra Press

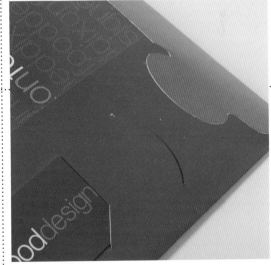

Think Pink

Who says one-color can't be fresh and savory? A delicious folder for Ed Dixon Food Design serves up the caterer's capabilities with flair. Designers at Flight Creative used a preexisting dieline and a limited palette to contain costs, but you'd never pick this as low-budget fare. The PMS pink is fully saturated on the cover and screened on the inside, where the caterer's logotype appears as a repeat pattern.

The folder, which accommodates A4 inserts such as menus and price quotes, was matte laminated for decadence and durability. Note the nonglued, puzzle-piece pocket tab.

Standing Tall

FreeMotion is a proprietary, strength-training system that simulates routine human activities such as pushing, pulling, lunging, and twisting. Unlike standard weight training equipment, which isolates individual muscles, FreeMotion engages complex muscle groups, building fitness for everyday life.

Just as FreeMotion represents a departure from the norm, so does its collateral. The brochure and folder are vertically oriented (the folder's center seam is actually along the top), much like the human body. A bold color palette and elongated forms reflect the physical attributes of the equipment itself. Powerful photography conveys a sense of movement.

COUNTRY	USA
DESIGN FIRM	Hornall Anderson Design Works
ART DIRECTORS	Jack Anderson & Kathy Saito
DESIGNERS	Kathy Saito, Sonja Max, Henry Yui, & Alan Copeland
PHOTOGRAPHER	Darrell Peterson
CLIENT	FreeMotion
PRINTER	Rainier Color

Connect the Dots

Printed material for an art and design college should be idiosyncratic, avant-garde, and even subversive. In designing a folder for Central Saint Martin's College, Marie Bertholle and Eric Gaspar decided to leave the cover copy up to the 1,500 students who would use the folder. The oversized jacket of corrugated cardstock is perforated with chads that aspiring creatives can punch out to create their own titles. The irony, of course, is that while the resulting aesthetic has the generic retro-tech appearance of a dot-matrix print job, there is nothing uniform about it.

The cost of the custom-perforated cover ended up claiming a large portion of the total folder budget, so the inside leaflet was printed in two colors with duotones for the photographs.

COUNTRIES	France/UK
DESIGN FIRM	EricandMarie
CREATIVE DIRECTORS	Marie Bertholle & Eric Gaspar
DESIGNERS	Marie Bertholle & Eric Gaspar
PHOTOGRAPHERS	Tomako Takasu & Holly Mackenzie
CLIENT	Central Saint Martin's College of Art and Design
PRINTER	Colortec

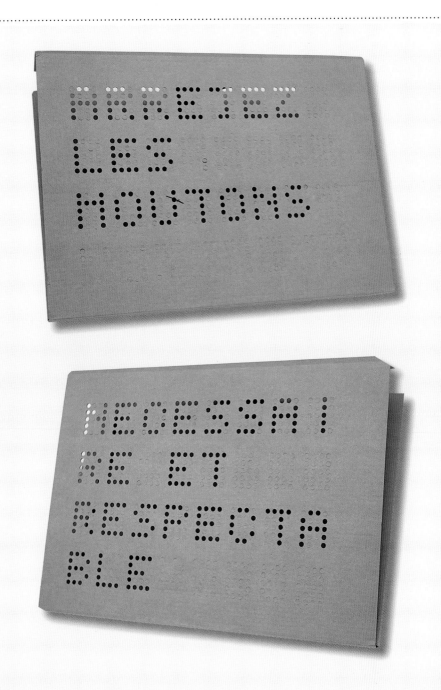

Wide-format Inkjet Production Printers

NUR
MACROPRINTERS

Pixel Perfect

If you're marketing state-of-the-art digital equipment to commercial printers, billboard media companies, and digital photo labs worldwide, your own printed materials had better be flawless. The folder system for NUR Macroprinters, a manufacturer of wide-format, inkjet printing systems, delivers.

On the cover, saturated color blocks resembling oversized pixels pop from a matte coated stock with a silver sheen. Square die-cuts in the folder cover create a seamless transition to the complementary materials inside. The middle capacity pocket is glued on both sides to create a secure satchel for bulky items. The side pocket sports a full bleed of neon orange on the back, which peeks through the cover windows when the folder is closed.

COUNTRY	Israel
DESIGN FIRM	Jason & Jason Visual Communication
CREATIVE DIRECTOR	Jonathan Jason
DESIGNER	Tamar Lourie
CLIENT	NUR Macroprinters
PRINTER	Yahalomi Zisman

On the Scene

The smoky, muscular identity for the production company Distrito Films alludes to its central location in the heart of Mexico City. The DF acronym coincides with the Mexican abbreviation for this city center, or *distrito federal.*

As a complement to the firm's urban-toned collateral, its heavyweight folder cover is a blank screen, adorned simply with a debossed graphic of the sans-serif logo and subtitled with a debossed, pearl foil stamp of the company name in small print. A combination of square and radius corners carries through every piece in the stationery system. The height of a die-cut in the folder pocket is tailored to bisect the vertical business card precisely at the waist.

COUNTRY	Mexico
DESIGN FIRM	Bløk Design
CREATIVE DIRECTOR	Vanessa Eckstein
DESIGNER	Vanessa Eckstein
CLIENT	Distrito Films
PRINTER	C. J. Graphics

Making Waves

Nordic Partners, a collaborative of investment banks in Norway, Sweden, and Finland, is a leading American broker-dealer specializing in investment opportunities in Scandinavia. The group's sales kit needed to underscore the clients' multinational presence. It also had to be flexible so that sales inserts could be easily updated.

Sharp Communications created an umbrella logo for the partnership, using colors that evoke the national flags of Norway, Sweden, and Finland. The logo mark's undulant shapes reference both Nordic and financial symbolism, suggesting notions of ocean waves or a bullhorn. Its sleek curves are repeated in the concave die-cut of the inside folder pocket and color-coded divider pockets. The folder stock is matte laminated for a smooth finish. A silver clasp serves as a stylish accessory, making it easy to swap out stale information and keep the contents fresh.

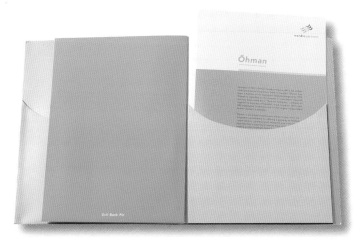

COUNTRIES	USA, Sweden, Norway, & Finland
DESIGN FIRM	Sharp Communications Inc.
CREATIVE DIRECTORS	Jim Brodsky & Anri Seki
DESIGNER	Anri Seki
COPYWRITER	Jim Brodsky
CLIENT	Nordic Partners
PRINTER	Peachtree Enterprises

In the Fold

When Siemens charged Baumann & Baumann with the redesign of its visual brand, the designers realized this was no ordinary, big-ticket corporate project. Whereas convention dictates that venerable brands are built on immutable type and color palettes, Siemens was open to a design system that would tread new paths, living in a constant state of organic metamorphosis and flux.

Consider that its graphic standards manual is not a bound document, but, rather, a variegated bouquet of eight folders, each offering graphic guidelines on subjects such as page layout, color palettes, paper finishes, typography, and PowerPoint formatting. The entire folder system nests in a nifty translucent poly box.

COUNTRY	Germany
DESIGN FIRM	Baumann & Baumann
CREATIVE DIRECTORS	Barbara & Gerd Baumann
DESIGNERS	Barbara & Gerd Baumann
CLIENT	Siemens AG
PRINTER	AWS Drucktechnik GmbH

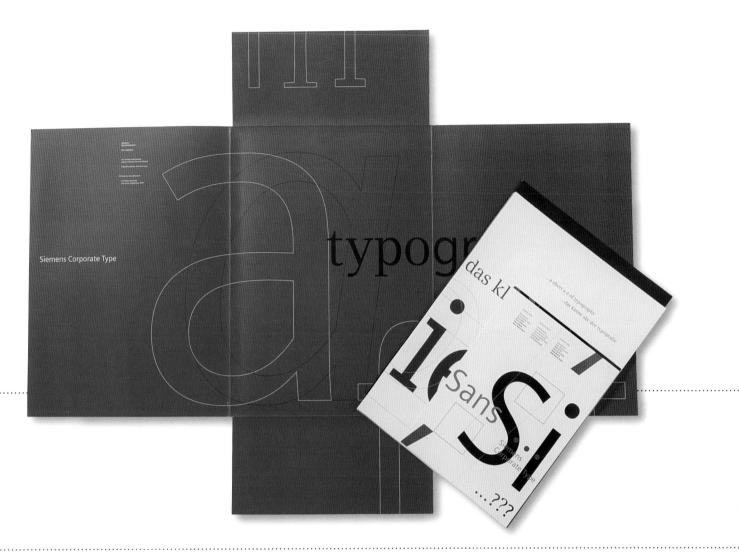

Heavy Duty

Entranco, a national engineering and consulting firm, wanted a marketing kit that would blow away the competition, setting a "Swiss Army knife" standard for modular print collateral.

Designed for maximum flexibility, the crisp, bold folder system reflects the firm's dynamic pragmatism; it can be customized to focus on a particular industry or service. A die-cut slot on the inside of the capacity folder holds custom-collated, spiral-bound presentations. Metal grommets and paper-clip accessories add industrial flavor, and the rectangular, die-cut notches that hold business cards resemble small buildings in relief. The whole package is held together with a thick, red, utilitarian rubber band printed with the company name.

COUNTRY	USA
DESIGN FIRM	Methodologie
CREATIVE DIRECTOR	Dale Hart
DESIGNER	Dale Hart
COPYWRITER	John Koval
CLIENT	Entranco
PRINTER	Cenveo Graphic Art Center

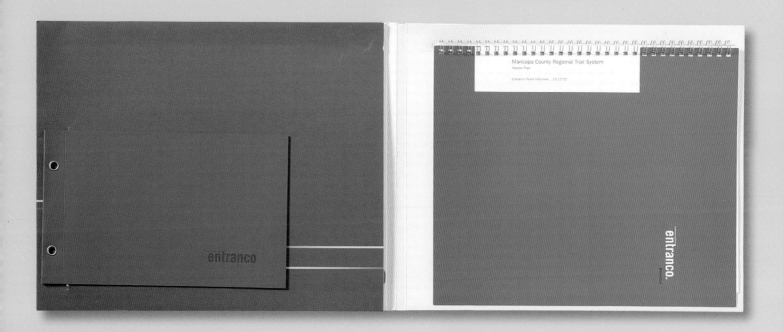

Aim High

Want an extradurable folder with a solid presence? Let the inside pockets do double duty. That was the solution Graphica devised in crafting its attention-grabbing, heavyweight promotional folder. Rather than bisecting the folder's inside pockets midpoint, designer Craig Terrones allowed them to run all the way to the top edge. Then he die-cut a rectangular chunk out of the inside corner of each pocket to offer a peek at matching inserts such as letterhead and case studies. Full floods of matte color on the pockets provide visual stability and make the inserts stand out.

The folder's spare cover directs the focus toward the studio's name and logo. Stout eyelets along the spine add a dimensional element and complement the logo's circular shape. They also bind four layers of 100 lb. (45 kg) cover-weight stock. The seams along the spine are scored to ensure that the folder lies flat when open.

COUNTRY	USA
DESIGN FIRM	Graphica
CREATIVE DIRECTOR	Craig Terrones
DESIGNER	Craig Terrones
CLIENT	Graphica
PRINTER	Cenveo Graphic Art Center

COUNTRY	Canada
DESIGN FIRM	Riordon Design
CREATIVE DIRECTOR	Ric Riordon
DESIGNER	Sharon Pece
CLIENT	Riordon Design
PRINTER	Contact Creative Services

House Blend

Riordon Design needed a versatile folder that could be used for new client pitches, as well as contract correspondence. Complementing the palette and aesthetic of the firm's letterhead, the folder features a crisp, embossed cover logo and a die-cut side tab for easily filing.

An uncoated stock gives the folder tactile appeal, and its bright surface pops in areas where reversed type is knocked out to white. For this reason, a premium paper sheet was worth the added expense. The free-fold pocket is die-cut and scored, but not glued (its side flaps fold inward to create an enclosure). This choice lent simplicity to the piece and saved money in bindery. Note the harmonious curved edges on the business cards and envelope flaps.

COUNTRY	Germany
DESIGN FIRM	Braue: Branding & Corporate Design
CREATIVE DIRECTOR	Kai Braue
DESIGNER	Annika Schmidt
COPYWRITERS	Annika Schmidt & Kai Braue
PHOTOGRAPHER	Harry Zier
CLIENT	Shin'Sei Chinesische Heilkunst
PRINTER	Druckhaus Wüst

Natural Curves

In the logo for Shin'Sei, a traditional Chinese medicine practice, young leaves sprout from a base of twiggy letterforms. The folder—an outgrowth of this aesthetic and part of a larger branding system—is constructed of natural, textured paper. The leaf shape proliferates not only in verdant photography but also in the organically curved pockets and flaps of the folder itself.

Because Shin'Sei treatment methods are rooted in traditional Chinese medicine, Braue specified traditional Chinese dimensions and formats for its collateral system, including the smaller, business-card size that is standard in China. To extend the folder's lifespan, the piece features a fold-up pocket flap with replaceable cards. The corners of the inserts and business card slots are all curved. Multiple dummies were created to ensure the overlapping motifs connected seamlessly. The closure for the folder, a sheer bellyband, circles the folder like a veil of mist.

Beauty Unfurled

In sculpting the identity for probeauty, a cosmetic surgery brand, Braue sought a sensitive and uplifting approach that would eclipse any thought of scalpels, tubes, and scars. The metamorphosis of a caterpillar into a butterfly provided a lyrical metaphor for aesthetic interpretation.

Every aspect of the brochure-folder is delicate and feminine. The piece has a shimmering luster and feels soft to the touch. Once opened, its side flaps unfold like the wings of a new butterfly. It took ten dummies to perfect the fold pattern for the die-cut wings. Early mock-ups had no closure, and the piece was prone to spring open. The locking clasp was eventually engineered to solve this problem.

COUNTRY	Germany
DESIGN FIRM	Braue: Branding & Corporate Design
CREATIVE DIRECTORS	Kai Braue & Marçel Robbers
DESIGNERS	Kai Braue & Marçel Robbers
CLIENT	probeauty
PRINTER	Druckerei Ditzen GmbH & Co. KG

Fast Track

Right-A-Way Applicators (RAW), a leading vegetation-control contractor serving railway systems in the US, needed a stationery system that would reflect its solid reputation and help it stand out from the competition.

RAW's bids for new contracts are submitted as written proposals, and, in most situations, constitute the first point of contact with prospective railway clients. A strong presentation folder and envelope convey a sense of precious cargo. The custom converted envelope features crisp letterpress scores and a peel-and-seal adhesive strip on the flap. As thematic subtext,

the envelope face is printed with a faint, tone-on-tone profile map of the largest rail yard in North America. This background pattern offsets the bold and straightforward RAW logo that is embossed and emblazoned in gloss foil on black custom folders.

The versatile folder system can hold anywhere from ten to one hundred sheets of paper, four business cards, and two company profiles. Die-cut notches along the top edges of insert sheets, business cards, and note cards are accented with embossed, wraparound labels resembling decorative railway ties.

COUNTRY	USA
DESIGN FIRM	So Design Co.
CREATIVE DIRECTOR	Aaron Pollock
DESIGNERS	Aaron Pollock & Mickey Smith
CLIENT	Right-A-Way Applicators
PRINTER	Diversified Graphics Inc.

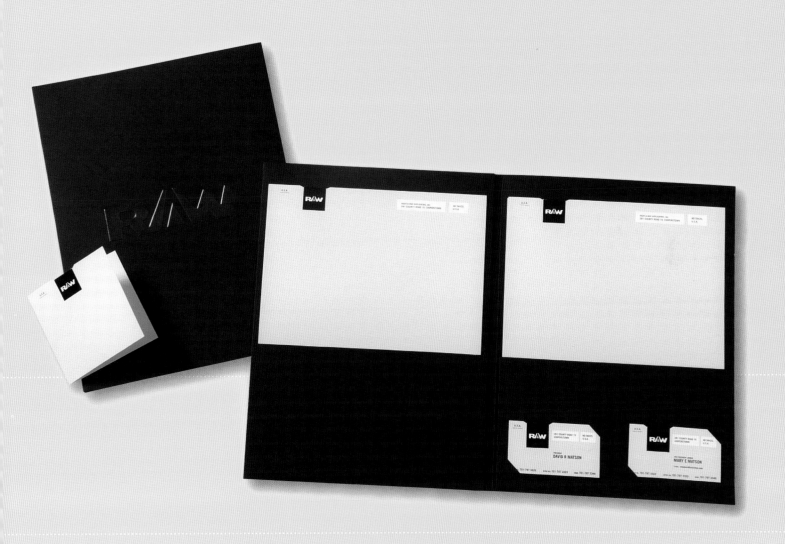

COUNTRY	USA
DESIGN FIRM	Rule29
CREATIVE DIRECTOR	Justin Ahrens
DESIGNER	Justin Ahrens
CLIENT	Mindware
PRINTER	O'Neil Printing

Points of Impact

Mindware, an electronic learning company offering Web, CD-ROM, and kiosk-based products, was a process-driven start-up. A volumetric logo represented the company's three proprietary, multipart processes, each comprising six components (hence, the hexagram shapes). Rule29 used these metaphorical shapes as a springboard for the construction of a memorable folder. The logo's angular edges were reiterated in the folder's pointed cover flap and triangular pocket folder. Portions of the logo also echoed in the outline of the business card, and the shape created when the business card was nested in the folder. The corners of the letterhead and business envelope flaps were similarly cropped to create a squared-off shape.

COUNTRIES	Indonesia / USA
DESIGN FIRM	AfterHours
CREATIVE DIRECTOR	Lans Brahmantyo
DESIGNER	Fedra Carina
CLIENT	AfterHours
PRINTER	Indonesia Printer

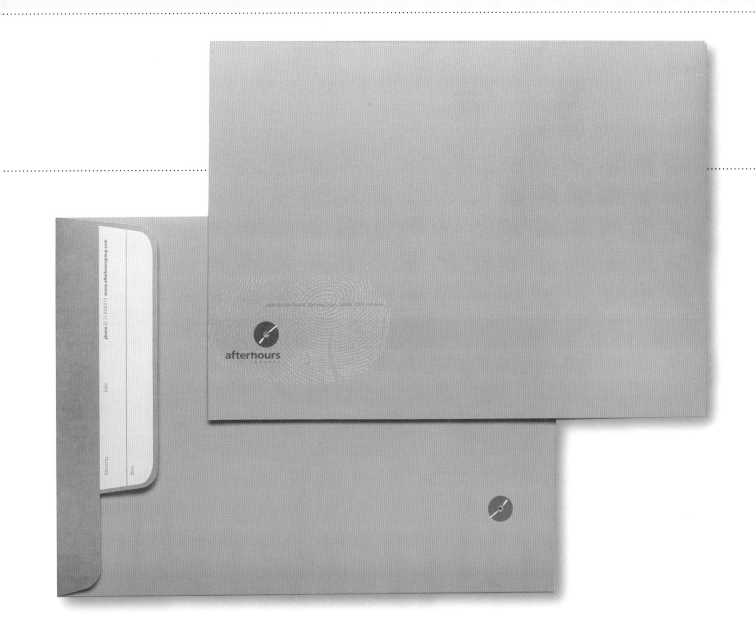

Conspicuous Carriers

AfterHours, a design firm with offices in Jakarta and Denver, wanted its envelopes to be highly visible and recognizable around town. Because 90 percent of its deliveries are local, postage costs were not a determinant. This allowed some savory unorthodoxy in the way of sizing.

Colors were a no-brainer. The tangy yellow and metallic silver representing the firm's identity provided a winning combo that promised to stand out on a crowded desk. The studio's signature die-cut tabs and punched

logomark were similarly applied to the envelope system to make it memorable. The big challenge was the minihole in the disk icon. The precision of the die-cut was critical, as the logo printed and punched through both sides of each envelope.

As evidence of the envelopes' contagious appeal, clients have been known to request them for their own use. By AfterHours' estimation, the pieces have become highly effective traveling advertisements.

On a Mission

REDF provides guidance, leadership, financial support, and training to a portfolio of nonprofit social enterprises in San Francisco. Its goal is to make nonprofit organizations more sustainable over time through business best practices and capacity building.

REDF only approaches high net-worth individuals who are able to invest a minimum of $150,000. Because of this, fund-raising materials targeting this group had to be sophisticated without appearing indulgent, so the two-color presentation folder was judiciously printed on just one side.

What the folder lacks in color it makes up for in texture; the stock is a velvety, cushiony, almost rubbery substrate (like neoprene) bound with a wide, translucent band.

An elegant, one-color direct mail piece is similarly distinctive, yet economical. Although the slate envelope was custom converted, the use of a prefabricated die (in a standard policy envelope size) kept costs in check.

COUNTRY	USA
DESIGN FIRM	Chen Design Associates
CREATIVE DIRECTOR	Joshua C. Chen
DESIGNERS	Max Spector & Joshua C. Chen
CLIENT	REDF
PRINTER	Oscar Printing Company

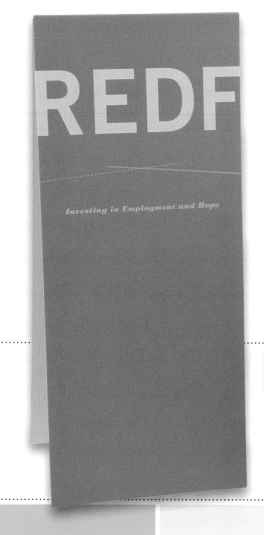

COUNTRY	USA
DESIGN FIRM	Bluelounge Design
CREATIVE DIRECTOR	Melissa Sunjaya
DESIGNER	Melissa Sunjaya
COPYWRITER	Kevin Kodama
CLIENT	Zoe Design Associates
PRINTER	Typecraft Wood & Jones

Fun with Functionality

Three-dimensional computer modeling is all in a day's work at Zoe Design Associates, an industrial design and product development firm in San Francisco. How could the studio's own pitch folder not have some dimension to it? The presentation system, created by Bluelounge Design, is light, airy, and heavy duty. Ethereal graphics on the cover convey a sense of levity, but the content becomes more substantive as the piece unfolds.

Clever pacing in the trifold design reveals a playful visual wit. At first glance, Zoe's company logo (on letterhead and business cards) peeks out from behind an angled pocket. The center panel then flips open to reveal another layer of goodies: a bold product brochure showcasing some of the firm's best projects.

For continuity, the folder is printed in Zoe's branded spot colors and features a combination of square and radius corners. Double capacity scores on all four sides turn the folder into a booklike entity with the studio name printed on one of the outside spines.

Fit to a Q

Hornall Anderson's first order of business was to devise the innovative name for aQuantive, a company specializing in Web analysis and marketing. Next came the witty brand identity. The design team's emphasis on the letter *Q* in the name is a nod to the qualitative and quantitative nature of the client's business. As a bisected letterform, the two halves of the *Q* become parentheses or brackets that symbolically house abstract forms suggesting data and bar codes.

The collateral folder features some choice nuances, such as business card tab slots that combine to create a reverse shape of the logo. Also of note is the innovative trifold capacity score down the folder's center spine, which allows it to be used flat or expanded to hold thicker inserts.

COUNTRY	USA
DESIGN FIRM	Hornall Anderson Design Works
ART DIRECTOR	Jack Anderson
DESIGNERS	Kathy Saito, Henry Yiu, Sonja Max, & Gretchen Cook
CLIENT	aQuantive Corp.
PRINTER	K/P Corporation

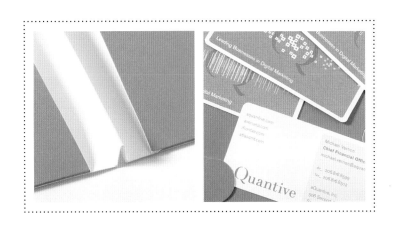

Full Disclosure

Elfen clients, upon receipt of the studio's stationery, would often ask, "What do you call that finish?" or "What kind of paper is this and can we print our job on the same thing?" The firm's owners, tired of repeating themselves, decided to print the production specifications directly on their letterhead, envelopes, business cards, and folders.

Papers and finishing techniques play the starring roles in this crisp, clean, paper system. The folder cover is unadorned, save a blind emboss of the studio's name at the bottom. As a complement to the foil-stamped business cards and foil mail pouch, the inside of the folder features a full bleed of silver metallic ink. The mailing envelope is sealed with a wraparound sticker label.

COUNTRY	UK
DESIGN FIRM	Elfen
CREATIVE DIRECTOR	Guto Evans
DESIGNER	Matthew James
CLIENT	Elfen
PRINTERS	Zenith Media & Hartley's Print

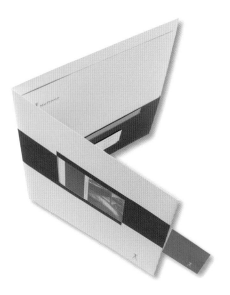

COUNTRY	USA
DESIGN FIRM	Rule29
CREATIVE DIRECTOR	Justin Ahrens
DESIGNERS	Justin Ahrens & Jon McGrath
PHOTOGRAPHER	MacDonald Photography
CLIENT	MacDonald Photography
PRINTER	O'Neil Printing

Film Strip

Photographer Brian MacDonald boasts a prolific range of subjects, including locations, products, and portraits. Rather than printing separate presentation folders for different kinds of clients, MacDonald wanted a flexible and modular system that could be inexpensively produced and customized.

Rule29's ingenious solution is a die-cut folder with a picture frame window, into which different style cards can be inserted. A folded panel of paper glued to the inside cover creates a pocket. Constructed of uncoated stock,

the two-color folder shell serves as an understated complement for each coated-stock photo card. Printing new cards in batches (in lieu of printing new folders) is not only economical, but it allows MacDonald to keep his promotions timely. The cards can be used as cover art in the folder, or separately as stand-alone direct mail pieces or handouts.

Inside the folder, a die-cut slot holds a square plastic sleeve and matching square note card. The plastic sleeve protects CDs of portfolio shots or purchased images that are being transferred to clients.

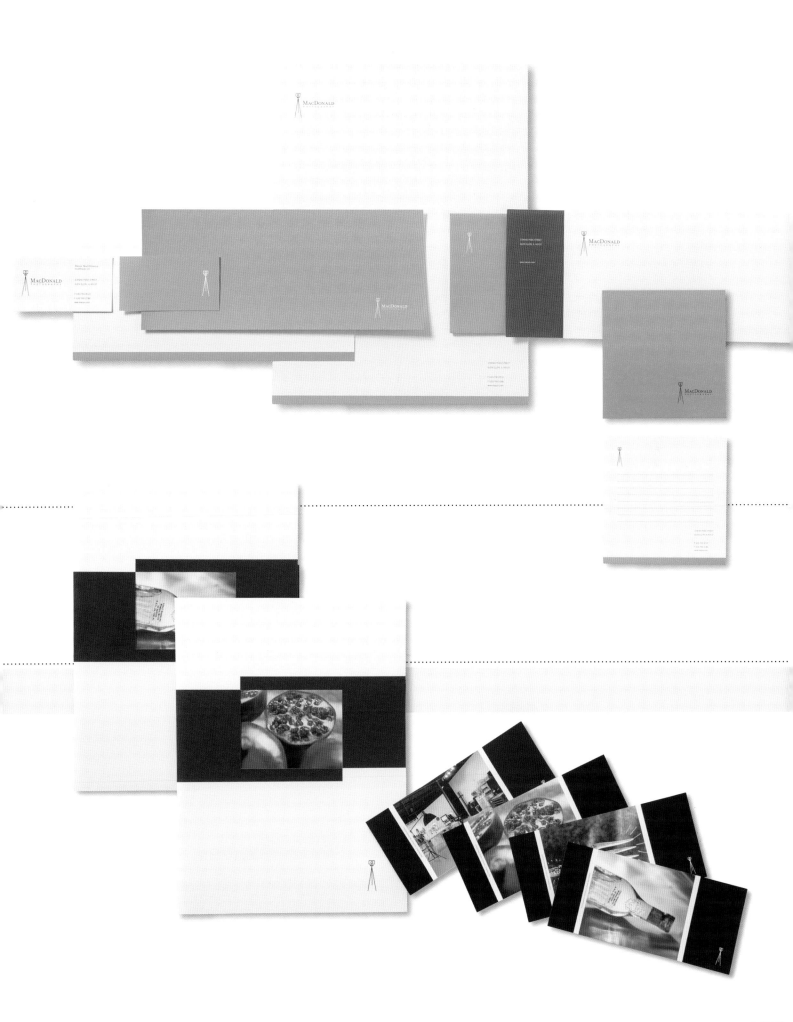

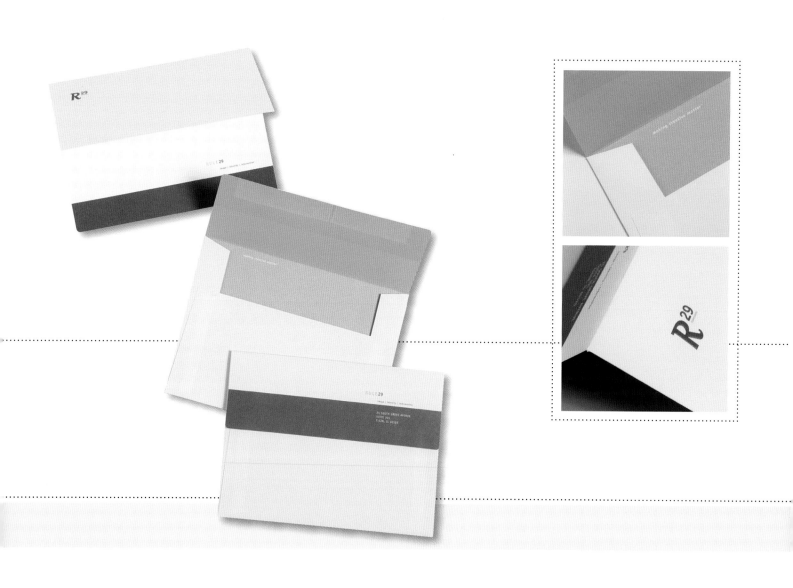

Overcoming the Paper Blues

On one hand, Rule29's stationery system is an exercise in restraint. The studio's pithy logo is a thread that runs throughout. On the other hand, indulgent variety comes in the system's prolific cornucopia of paper stocks. Incorporating multiple papers posed a significant production challenge, in that the firm's signature PMS colors printed differently on different substrates. The printer ended up having to mix custom inks to match each paper.

The studio's custom folder is a refreshing bright white, simply adorned with an embossed logo and a tab-slot closure on the cover. Stacked die-cuts on the inside show off letterhead, business cards, and envelopes on variegated stocks.

Rule29's tagline, "Making creative matter" is especially poignant when rendered small in carefully chosen spots. It's the first message one sees upon tearing open the envelope flap.

COUNTRY	USA
DESIGN FIRM	Rule29
CREATIVE DIRECTOR	Justin Ahrens
DESIGNER	Justin Ahrens
CLIENT	Rule29
PRINTER	O'Neil Printing

A Fashionable Address

The Residence is a magnificent, $10 million (£5.3 million) penthouse condominium development in the heart of Toronto's pulsating financial and fashion district, with neighbors including Prada, Gucci, and Tiffany & Co.

The marketing package touting the property is equally *de rigueur*. An iridescent pewter envelope is luxuriously debossed for tactile flair. Floor plan inserts wrapped in an effervescent orange, silk-coated cover, peek smartly from the edge like a crisp shirtsleeve at the cuff of a fine suit. Handsome letter-pressed invitations and a sleek brochure are tailored to match.

COUNTRY	Canada
DESIGN FIRM	52 Pick-up Inc.
CREATIVE DIRECTORS	Nick Monteleone & Susan McIntee
DESIGNERS	Nick Monteleone & Susan McIntee
CLIENT	Tridel Corporation
PRINTER	Somerset

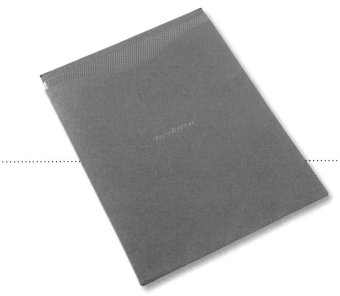

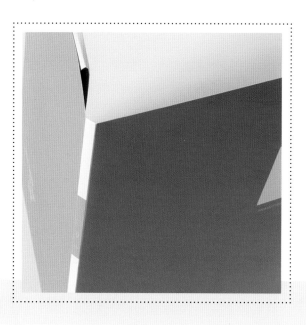

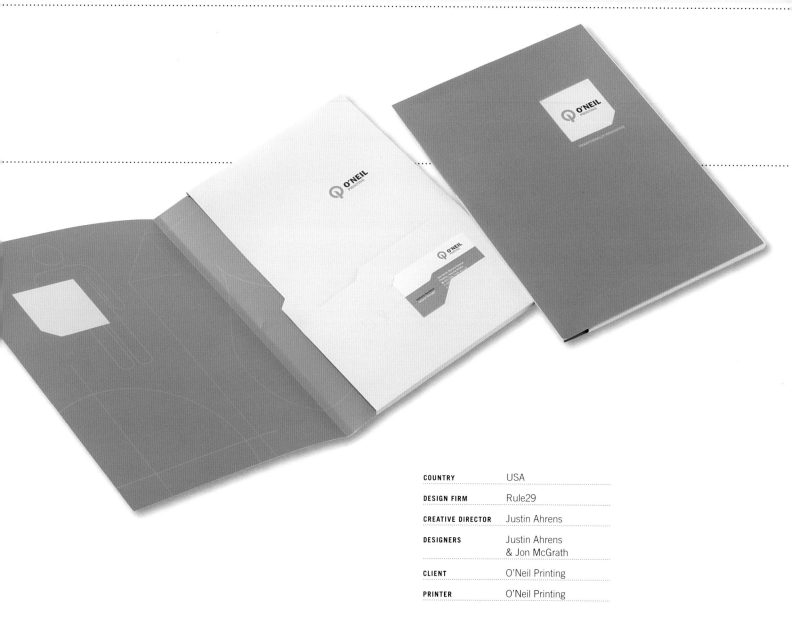

COUNTRY	USA
DESIGN FIRM	Rule29
CREATIVE DIRECTOR	Justin Ahrens
DESIGNERS	Justin Ahrens & Jon McGrath
CLIENT	O'Neil Printing
PRINTER	O'Neil Printing

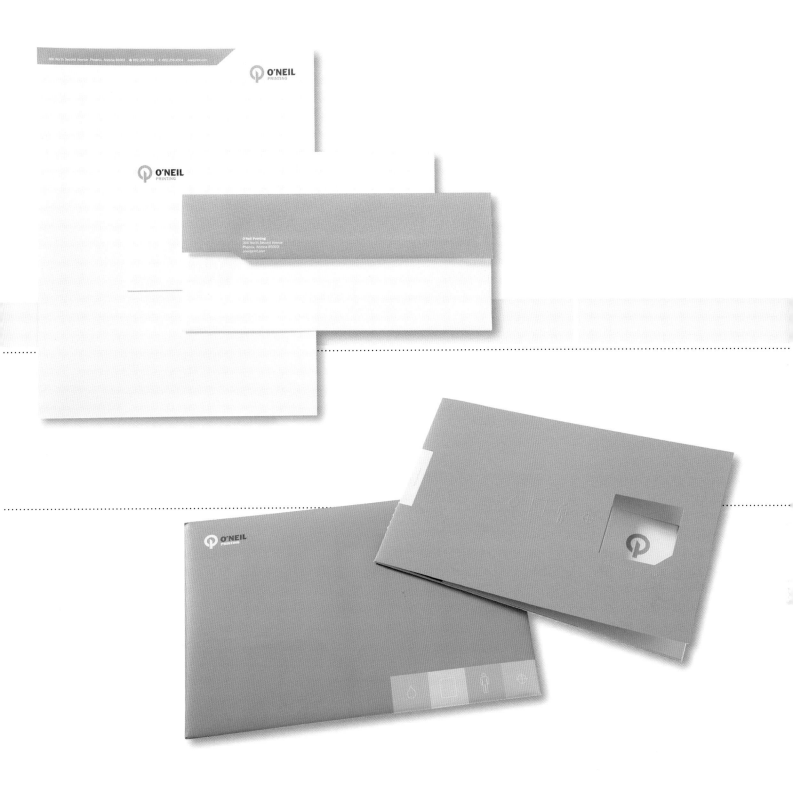

Up a Notch

A dated appearance can be the death of a printer. After ninety-five years in business, O'Neil Printing needed a facelift and commissioned a new logo. Shortly thereafter, the venerable company hired Rule29 to apply its fresh visage to a range of promotional materials.

Details delight in the collateral. The logo's angular blade shape resonates subtly throughout—in die-cut envelope flaps, folder pockets, and business card slots. O'Neil's signature blue is liberally spread as a full bleed on oversized delivery envelopes and folder interiors. Its crisp icon system serves both navigational and decorative functions. On the spine of the capacity folder, the tiny icons read like a book imprint label. Inside the folder, they function as screened illustrations, adding linear texture to an otherwise flat field of color.

Silver Metal Winner

Labels offer an interesting and relatively inexpensive means of adding texture and pizzazz to a mail piece. A promotional mailer for Leading Label Company proves it. The custom foil envelope—specified to match the silver PMS color in the company's identity system—begs attention when it lands on the desks of designers and print brokers. Colors and motifs lifted from the collateral inside are foreshadowed in crisp labels on the outside of the metallic mailer. The labels are blind embossed, adding a "must touch" factor to each delivery.

To sell his idea to the client, designer Alex Lloyd constructed an elaborate mock-up. This included a faux-embossed, one-off label, which he created manually by printing out the graphic, gluing it to heavy cardstock, carving out the image with a scalpel, arranging the pieces on cellotape to hold them in position, and then overlaying the relief design with soft paper and making a rubbing with a stylus.

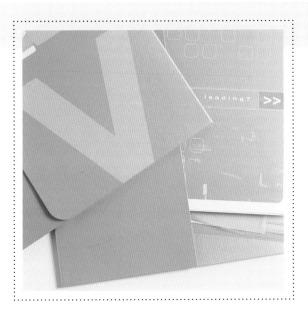

COUNTRY	New Zealand
DESIGN FIRM	Lloyds Graphic Design Ltd.
CREATIVE DIRECTOR	Alexander Lloyd
CLIENT	Leading Label Co.
PRINTER	Chaucer Press

COUNTRY	UK
DESIGN FIRM	Blue River Design Ltd.
CREATIVE DIRECTOR	Cathy Graham
SENIOR DESIGNER	Cathy Graham
ACCOUNT MANAGER	Anthony Cantwell
CLIENT	Baltic Centre for Contemporary Art
PRINTER	Team Impression Ltd.

Art Smart

Baltic is an international contemporary art center situated on the banks of the River Tyne in Gateshead, England. The center functions as a public art space and "art factory" where artists from across the globe come to work and exhibit. Mailings are an important part of the center's image. A bold, industrial stationery system is central to establishing cobranding partnerships with large corporations.

A durable cardstock forms the basis for a family of versatile folders and envelopes. Like a gallery wall, the stationery is intentionally neutral so as not to interfere with the art. The square capacity folder with a die-cut slot closure makes a fine shell for glossy photo cards. A capacity policy envelope—scored along the sides and end flap so that it can be used flat, or expanded to hold bulkier inserts—is secured with a sticker seal for an official feel. Other envelopes and sleeves in alternate sizes complement the branding system.

COUNTRY	Mexico
DESIGN FIRM	Bløk Design
CREATIVE DIRECTOR	Vanessa Eckstein
DESIGNER	Vanessa Eckstein
CLIENT	Centro
PRINTER	Artes Graficas Panorama

WHY
STUDY
AT
THE
CENTR

The Centro is the first institution for hig
in Mexico specializing in cinema, televisic
munication, new media, and design. The
four degree programs based on an inte
approach and developed according to the
regarding both content and methodology
striving to provide academic and profess
lence within our degree programs we a
committed to continuing education, researc
and dissemination. The Centro's facilities,
human talent are dedicated to making it the
for students to freely express and develop the
energy and professional potential.

EXIT   mobiliario

cen

Surprise on the Outside

Capturing the attention of prospective students at a bustling recruitment fair is no easy task—especially if you are a new and relatively unknown design school with a limited budget. Bløk Design's thrifty solution for Centro squeezed extra mileage out of a poster the firm had already designed for the university. The print run of the poster was increased, and the extra posters were converted into eye-catching envelopes. Because the envelopes were randomly cut, no two were alike. As a result, each bore a sense of dynamism and surprise. Odd dimensions (determined by the poster size) and extra long glue flaps added quirky appeal.

Specifying an economical bond paper for the poster-envelopes freed up funds for more ink colors on press. The taupe and turquoise palette complements the university's sleek and modular identity system. Note the innovative use of end flaps in lieu of diagonal seams on the stationery envelopes.

Bundles of Joy

Wendy and Amy were new moms wanting to streamline the process of sending baby pictures to faraway family and friends. They asked Gillespie Design to create a stylish self-mailer that would cradle photos through the postal system unscathed. The duo's motives were also entrepreneurial. They wanted a cute identity and packaging system that could be sold at the retail level.

Several weeks later, a set of bouncing baby photo carriers was born. Inside each durable capacity booklet, a plump, cloud-shaped caption panel provides space to jot a note. Opposite, a pocket with a matching, scalloped edge holds up to six photo prints. Each piece is held closed with a clear wafer seal. The color choices—sage or tangerine—are gender neutral and a fresh departure from traditional baby hues. Another smart detail? The stamp spot indicates the amount of first class postage needed, depending on the number of photos inside.

COUNTRY	USA
DESIGN FIRM	Gillespie Design
CREATIVE DIRECTOR	Maureen Gillespie
DESIGNER	Liz Schenkel
CLIENT	Wendy and Amy
PRINTER	Dejay Litho

COUNTRY	UK
DESIGN FIRM	Aloof Design Ltd.
CREATIVE DIRECTOR	Sam Aloof
DESIGNER	Chris Barham
CLIENT	Georgina Goodman
PRINTER	Paul Haslam/ Benwel Sebard Ltd.
PAPER	GFSmith

A Bespoke Package

When couture designer Georgina Goodman opened a London showroom for fine shoes and accessories, Aloof Design was asked to create a range of fine packaging materials for in-store and promotional use. Inspiration for the luxurious, debossed "glove envelope" (it holds scarves as well) was drawn from Parisienne boutique packaging and from the designer's upscale shoe collection.

Paper mock-ups in a range of weights and finishes allowed the design team to its their concept before arriving at the envelope's final form. A matte laminate was added to one side of a premium uncoated stock for durability—its finish resembling the natural texture of the leather hide from which the shoes themselves are made.

The only hiccup in the process involved the die-cut holes for the ribbon closure. The team originally intended for the two sets of holes to be the same size, but due to the nature of the die-cutting process, the holes would not have aligned. To overcome this problem, the holes on the body of the envelope were made a few millimeters larger, with the smaller holes in the flap fitting perfectly over top when the flap is closed.

The glove envelope is part of a larger branding system that includes bags, shoeboxes, swing tickets, business cards, printed tissue paper, and debossed stationery.

COUNTRY	USA
DESIGN FIRM	And Partners
CREATIVE DIRECTOR	David Schimmel
DESIGNER	David Schimmel
CLIENT	And Partners
PRINTERS	Piccani Press & COE Display

Drawing Attention

The average design firm promo includes at least five portfolio samples showcasing the studio's abilities. And Partners had only one annual report to show—one that it served up with humor and pride. The show-and-tell package featuring its annual report for VF Corporation also included four blank dummies symbolizing its annual report projects of the future.

The quirky package also included an illustrated booklet of explanation, inspired by Mad Libs, tracing books, and airport travel games for kids. The booklet's take on the number five was foreshadowed in a sequence of hands printed on the stock bubble wrap envelope mailer. The book was limited to one color to control costs, but the piece was still colorful. A fat, red rubber band (used to hold the contents together) complements the envelope's thin Ziploc seal and provides a punchy accent.

Rabbit Run

Prank Design's very first promo piece had its sights set on the music business—a realm where subversive stunts and all varieties of weirdness are reverentially appreciated. Its package of goodies read like an oddball prize retrieved from a gumball machine. The kit was hand-stapled and sent to prospective clients in an off-the-shelf chipboard mailer.

To elevate each mailer beyond the generic, the Prank guys silk-screened their logo (a jackalope) onto the chipboard surface, creating a white area for the mailing address. The screen-printing phase was completed in a single evening for a mere $40. The big time outlay came later, in the ornate hand lettering of each recipient's address.

COUNTRY	USA
DESIGN FIRM	Prank Design
CREATIVE DIRECTORS	Michael Crigler & Robb Ogle
DESIGNER	Michael Crigler
CLIENT	Prank Design
PRINTER	Prank Design (In-house)

The Cat's Meow

Maiow Creative was moving to a new space and simultaneously reinventing its look. The new identity featured a repetitive, origami-style pattern evoking the studio's Japanese heritage. In the clever moving notice, the odd-shaped envelope is the announcement. The entire piece unfolds into a poster.

Maiow deliberately broke the rules and specified a thin stock—bible paper, in fact—to prevent its one-color layout from appearing flat and boring.

Several printers refused to quote the job because they were reluctant to put heavy ink coverage on such a light sheet. But the gamble paid off. The result is an interesting interaction between the two translucent sides of the poster-mailer. The studio also printed a quantity of the poster sheets only on one side. These sheets are used for presentations, wrapping paper, and packing material.

COUNTRY	UK
DESIGN FIRM	Maiow Creative Branding
CREATIVE DIRECTOR	Paul Rapacioli
DESIGNERS	Paul Rapacioli, Ceri Lewis, & Dave Worthington
CLIENT	Maiow Creative Branding
PRINTER	Good News

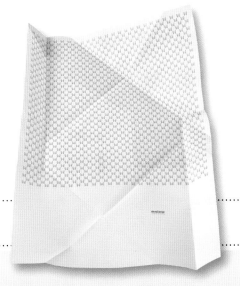

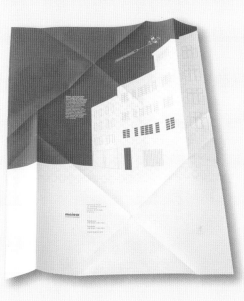

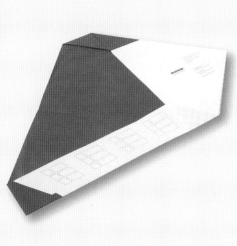

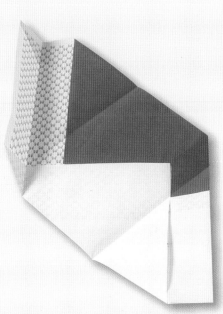

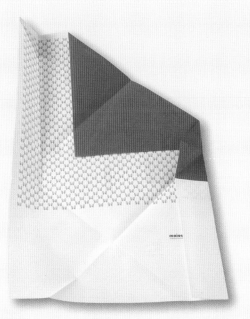

Graphic Exposure

Designer Shinnoske Sugisaki was preparing for a gallery exhibition
in Osaka and needed a compelling promotional mailer. A transparent
vellum envelope acts as a coquettish veil for a preview of the artist's
work. Japanese characters printed on the envelope created a layered
effect with the English text on the catalog underneath.

Sugisaki worked with the printer to choose papers and inks that allowed
the linear cover graphic to pop from inside the envelope. Thermography
was used to create a shiny, dimensional surface. Tinted inks create
a robust plane of fire engine red.

COUNTRY	Japan
DESIGN FIRM	Shinnoske Inc.
ART DIRECTOR	Shinnoske Sugisaki
DESIGNERS	Shinniske Sugisaki, Chiaki Okuno, & Shinsuke Suzuki
CLIENT	Ban Gallery
PRINTER	Asahi Seihan Printing Co. Ltd.

Friendly Face

When Sayles Graphic Design hired Melissa Marchant as its new studio manager, the firm celebrated her arrival by hosting a "Hello" party. Clients, vendors, and friends were invited to come on down and meet the newest member of the team.

A generic nametag served as the springboard for the invitation concept. The studio logo peers through the big, bold *O* in the die-cut envelope.

COUNTRY	USA
DESIGN FIRM	Sayles Graphic Design
CREATIVE DIRECTOR	John Sayles
DESIGNER	John Sayles
ILLUSTRATOR	John Sayles
COPYWRITER	Wendy Lyons
CLIENT	Sayles Graphic Design
PRINTER	Action Print

Turbo Prop

Volvo Aero, a manufacturer of high-tech components for aircraft, rocket, and gas turbine engines, was hosting a chalet at the Farnborough International Air Show. The company hoped for a full house, so it issued boarding passes. An invitation resembling an airline ticket slid inside a custom converted itinerary sleeve, which was then mailed in a silver-gray translucent envelope to client partners and prospects.

Several dummies were created in advance to test paper choices. Heavy ink coverage on the semigloss, text-weight invitation jacket required an extra day to dry. Volvo Aero mailed 3,000 invitations and received 2,956 RSVP cards in return.

COUNTRIES	Sweden/USA/UK
DESIGN FIRM	Pinpoint Communications
CREATIVE DIRECTOR	Leonel Diaz
CLIENT	Volvo Aero
PRINTER	H&D Graphics

COUNTRY	USA
DESIGN FIRM	Greteman Group
CREATIVE DIRECTOR	Sonia Greteman
DESIGNER	James Strange
COPYWRITER	Raleigh Drennon
CLIENT	Bombardier Aerospace
PRINTER	Donlevy Lithograph

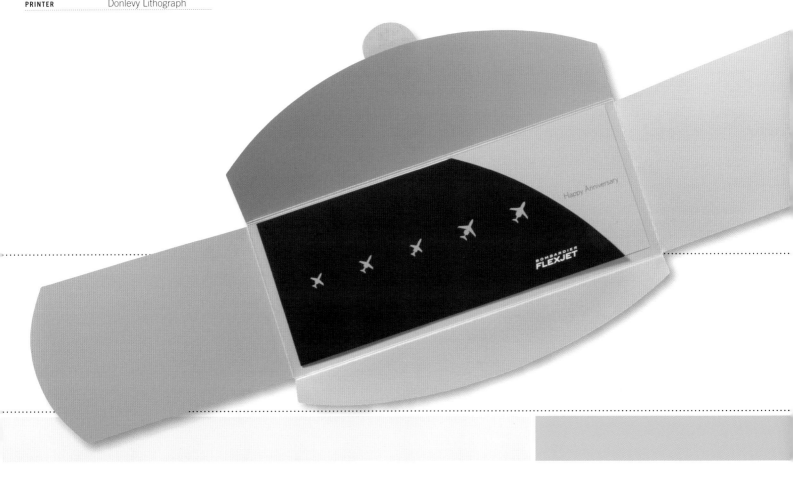

Jet Set

A plain envelope wouldn't have done justice to the clever announcement heralding the tenth anniversary of Bombardier's Flexjet. The card's crisp, concave edge smartly resembles an airplane nose, and its cover graphics (a succession of planes) read like windows lining a fuselage. An oversized custom envelope with wing flaps is the perfect anatomical complement.

Metallic and jet black inks make a luxurious impression in this upscale piece sent to affluent plane buffs and corporate patrons. A vintage inspired seal on the inside of the card matches the sticker closure on the outside of the envelope.

COUNTRY	USA
DESIGN FIRM	IE Design + Communications
CREATIVE DIRECTOR	Marcie Carson
DESIGNER	Jane Kim
CLIENT	BMW of North America
PRINTERS	Classic Litho & Roadrunner Press

Mini Masterpiece

BMW's Mini Masters Council was an exclusive event for the Mini brand's top salespeople. An e-ticket, luggage tag, and contact card were included in the first mailing to 150 participants. The second mailing had an equally diminutive print run and a small budget to match. IE Design was challenged to engineer a high-end, attention-grabbing promo within these parameters.

The result is a delightful little 9.5" X 4.5" (24 X 11 cm) pocket folder that fits like a glove inside a matching envelope sleeve. Coated and uncoated papers are punched up with spot gloss and dull varnishes to create visual texture. The winged Mini logo on the folder cover peeks through a die-cut window in the envelope.

Not Standard Issue

The Dockers K-1 Khakis line was inspired by the original khakis developed for the US army in the 1930s. Hang tags and other K-1 brand accessories evoke the nostalgia of that era, incorporating raw industrial materials, silk-screening, and letterpress printing.

In the retail world, "pant flashers" are usually simple offset-printed cards that attach to the pocket and identify the brand. Templin Brink's approach allows the brand to leave more of a lasting imprint. A parchment-colored, letter-pressed envelope contains an intimate little storybook chronicling the history of khakis. The envelope is hole-punched and attached to the trousers with a metal chain. The utilitarian aesthetic is reminiscent of vintage dog tags. It commands attention.

COUNTRY	USA
DESIGN FIRM	Templin Brink Design
CREATIVE DIRECTOR	Gaby Brink
DESIGNER	Gaby Brink
CLIENT	Dockers
PRINTER	KEA Inc.

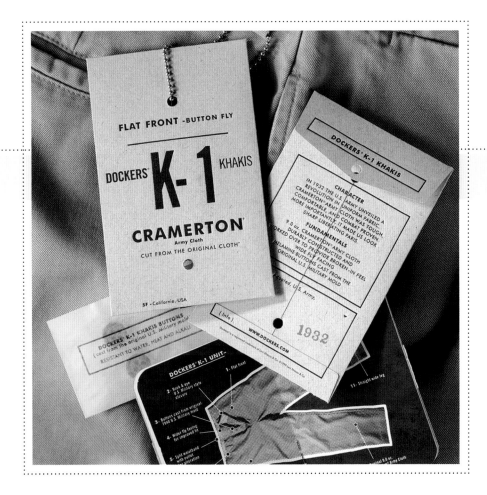

Roundabout Way

In redesigning their own identity system, the creative team at BBK Studio had a craving for radius corners to give the stationery an extra dose of style. The challenge was creating a #10 envelope with a rounded face to match the curved letterhead and note cards. Achieving this subtle effect meant die-cutting a wedge into either side of the seam joining the envelope's main body to its flap. The curves of the die-cut needed to blend perfectly into the straight sides of envelopes that had already been converted.

Several hand prototypes were made to arrive at a dieline that wasn't deep enough to allow the corners of the letters to stick out, or to cause jamming in postal processing equipment. The team mailed test correspondence around the country to make sure the postal service wouldn't put a kibosh on its plan. The end result was a tasty package with a double hit of orange on the inside of the envelope.

COUNTRY	USA
DESIGN FIRM	BBK Studio
CREATIVE DIRECTOR	Yang Kim
DESIGNERS	Yam Kim & Kevin Budelmann
CLIENT	BBK Studio
PRINTER	Foremost Graphics

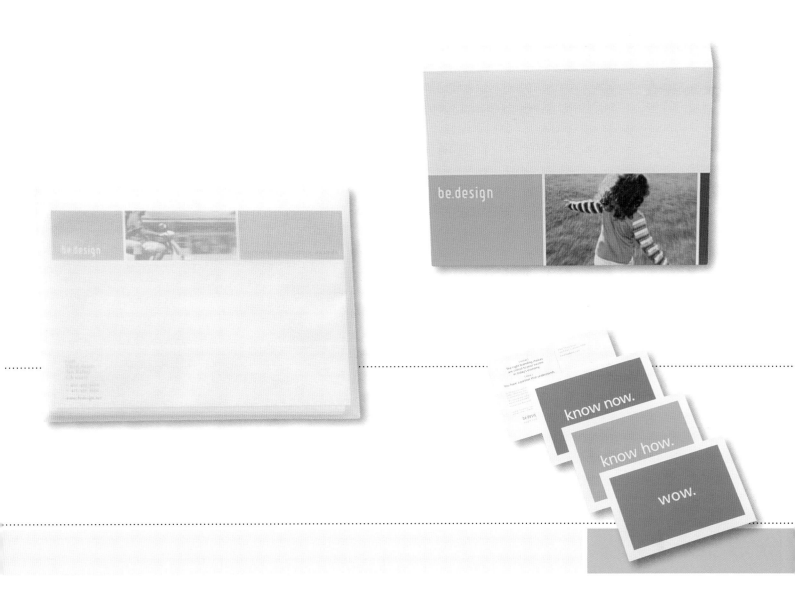

COUNTRY	USA
DESIGN FIRM	Be Design
CREATIVE DIRECTORS	Will Burke & Eric Read
DESIGNERS	Yusuke Asaka, Shinichi Eguchi, & Jeff Martel
COPYWRITER	Deborah Read
PHOTOGRAPHER	Richard Eskite
CLIENT	Be Design
PRINTER	Paragraphics

Shining Through

Be Design wanted to showcase its talents while illustrating its ability to "see things through." A 6" X 9" (15 X 22.5 cm) mailer does the job in style. The translucent envelope (purchased off the shelf) offers an instant sneak peek at the studio's work. Inside, the firm's capabilities and branding savvy are highlighted on a set of pithy mix-and-match cards.

The design team spent a little extra for an envelope stock that was both sturdy and transparent. They saved money on printing by ganging the four-color postcards in tandem with another job. Using a standard postcard size helped minimize postage costs.

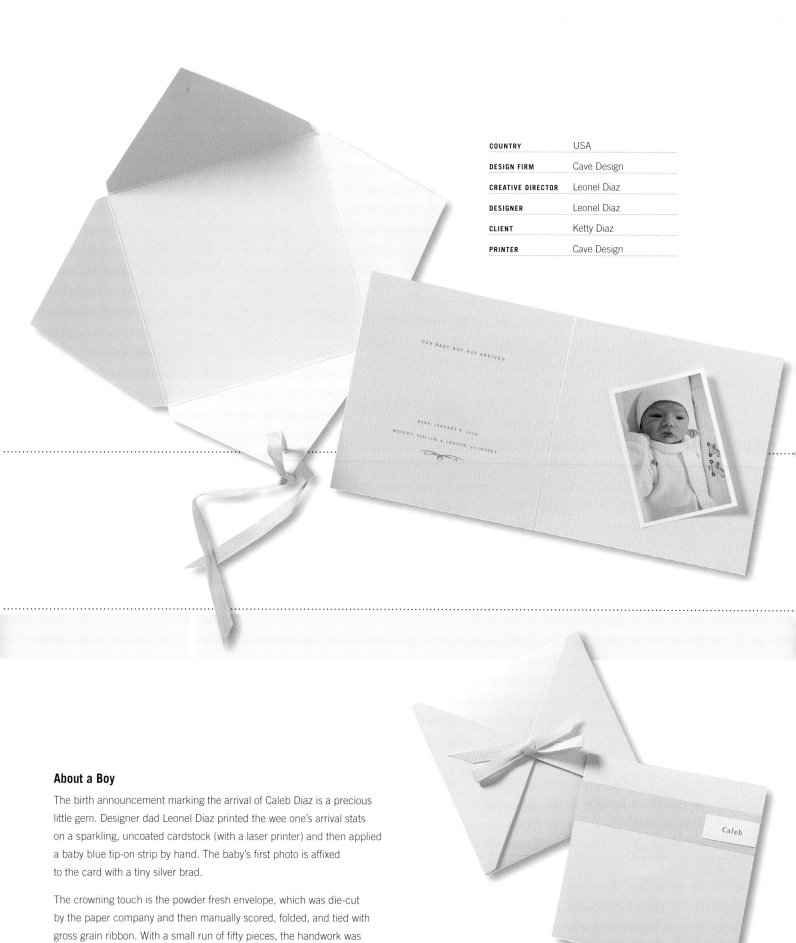

COUNTRY	USA
DESIGN FIRM	Cave Design
CREATIVE DIRECTOR	Leonel Diaz
DESIGNER	Leonel Diaz
CLIENT	Ketty Diaz
PRINTER	Cave Design

About a Boy

The birth announcement marking the arrival of Caleb Diaz is a precious little gem. Designer dad Leonel Diaz printed the wee one's arrival stats on a sparkling, uncoated cardstock (with a laser printer) and then applied a baby blue tip-on strip by hand. The baby's first photo is affixed to the card with a tiny silver brad.

The crowning touch is the powder fresh envelope, which was die-cut by the paper company and then manually scored, folded, and tied with gross grain ribbon. With a small run of fifty pieces, the handwork was manageable. The whole piece mailed in a clear plastic bag.

Flower Power

Inspiration for Nassar Design's coquettish 2004 holiday card was drawn from "La Vie en Rose," the World War II–era song made legendary by chanteuse Edith Piaf. The crimson metallic envelope is custom die-cut in the shape of an open flower to emphasize the double meaning of the theme in French: a rosy life, as well as a life with roses. The envelope is flat on one side and pops up into a dimensional object on the other— making it, in the words of Roland Barthes, both subject and object.

A silver-scripted message on the card enclosure encourages the recipient to "wear the year lightly as a feather," and an actual feather applique refers to Piaf's songbird status. The envelope flaps are letterpress scored, folded, and held closed with a matching foil sticker.

COUNTRY	USA
DESIGN FIRM	Nassar Design
CREATIVE DIRECTOR	Nelida Nassar
DESIGNERS	Nelida Nassar & Margarita Encomienda
COPYWRITER	Helen Goddard
PHOTOGRAPHER	Nassar Design
PRINTER	Alpha Press

On the Move

Communication Visual was relocating from Florida to Washington, D.C., and expanding the scope of its client base. Creating a new capabilities piece was an important part of the transition, but the return address was a question mark. Unsure where exactly they would land in their new hometown, partners Galen and Julie Lawson opted for an accordion-fold self-mailer that could be delivered flat, assembled in-house, and sealed shut with a return address label generated by an office laser printer.

Part brochure, part folder, and part envelope, the hybrid piece features folded tabs that cradle interchangeable postcard inserts. The package closes with a tab/slot system. Its only drawback? The cardstock shell is scored for extra capacity, but the box shape sometimes gets flattened in the mail.

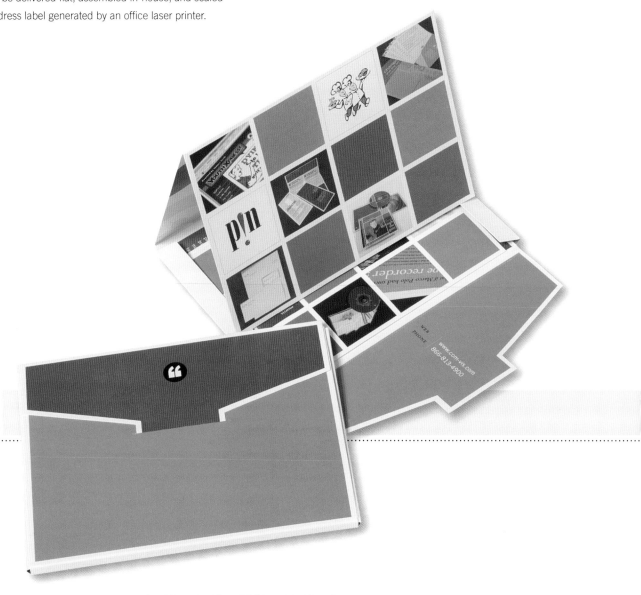

COUNTRY	USA
DESIGN FIRM	Communication Visual
CREATIVE DIRECTOR	Galen Lawson
DESIGNER	Galen Lawson
COPYWRITER	Julie Lawson
PHOTOGRAPHER	Riku/I Anna
CLIENT	Communication Visual
PRINTER	Spectrum Printing

Navigational Aid

Showcase Canada was a tradeshow concept promoting corporate travel from New York to the Great White North. An innovative invitation points the way. The folder opens on all sides and unfurls into a compass shape, with a flag-red flap (loosely resembling an *N*) pointing due north.

The folder's pinwheel construction offered a unique housing for the invitation, reply card, and reply envelope. It was also cost effective, in that the small side flaps made it possible to die-cut the whole piece in a single pass with a perimeter cut.

Following the success of the New York promo, the Showcase Canada concept was introduced to corporate travel planners in Boston and Hartford.

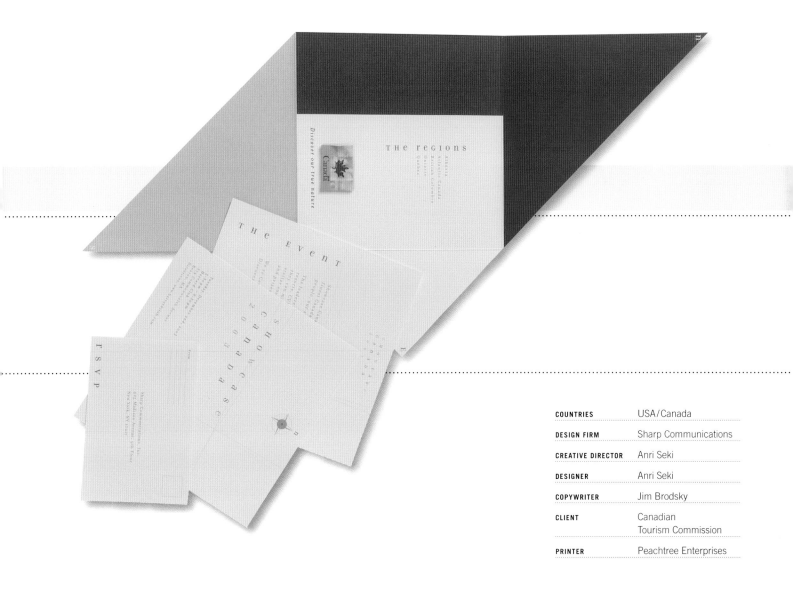

COUNTRIES	USA/Canada
DESIGN FIRM	Sharp Communications
CREATIVE DIRECTOR	Anri Seki
DESIGNER	Anri Seki
COPYWRITER	Jim Brodsky
CLIENT	Canadian Tourism Commission
PRINTER	Peachtree Enterprises

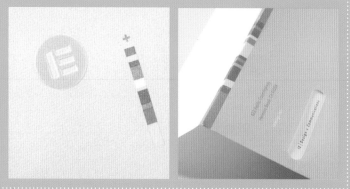

Fair Trade

After nine years in business, IE Design was all grown up and moving to new digs. No longer a boutique shop, the design firm needed a new identity to reflect its seasoned expertise and growing size as well as the physical characteristics of the remodeled space it was about to inhabit. Funds for new stationery were limited, given that a considerable sum had been allocated to the build-out.

IE's studio space opens with a splash of bright white and becomes progressively muted as the space recedes. This tonal continuum is reflected in a stationery system that is both simple and sophisticated. To keep its price tag from skyrocketing, IE bartered design services in exchange for free offset printing. The flat press sheets were sent to a finisher for embossing, foil stamping, cutting, scoring, folding, and converting.

Choice details in the stationery system include a rounded, die-cut window in the envelope (which allows the return address to peek through from the letterhead) and embossed, pearl-metallic, foil-stamped logos on the letterhead and envelope flap. The stripe pattern along the top of the envelope smartly wraps from front to back. This decision prevented a scenario in which the pattern almost—but didn't quite—line up perfectly with the envelope fold.

COUNTRY	USA
DESIGN FIRM	IE Design + Communications
CREATIVE DIRECTOR	Marcie Carson
DESIGNER	Marcie Carson
CLIENT	IE Design + Communications
PRINTERS	Inland Litho & Burdge Inc.

COUNTRY	UK
DESIGN FIRM	Pemberton and Whitefoord Design
CREATIVE DIRECTOR	Simon Pemberton
DESIGNER	Simon Pemberton
PHOTOGRAPHER	James Murphy
CLIENT	James Murphy
PRINTER	Burlington Press
BOX MANUFACTURER	Box and Bag Man Ltd.

Photo Matte

What better way to transport photographic prints than in a sturdy photo paper box? A promo mailer for food photographer James Murphy does just that. A delectable brochure with an embossed, die-stamped, rubber cover nests inside a box envelope designed to resemble a sheath of photo paper—complete with a branded sticker label to prevent product tampering. Covered with a textured matte paper, the envelope provides understated contrast to the high-gloss photos inside.

The mailer was custom sized and converted to match the dimensions of an actual photo paper box. Some of the boxes bowed after they were covered in the matte paper and had to be discarded.

Structural Integrity

Superlative architecture often involves a delightful integration of art and engineering, nature and structure. A catalog for an architecture exhibition at the Royal College of Art carries this mantra to print. Not satisfied with the creative limitations of an A5 envelope, designers Marie Bertholle and Eric Gaspar found a way to go bigger.

The oversized catalog cover, which wraps around the book and doubles as an envelope, reads as a metaphorical land map. When open, the cover builds a large surface around the book, like a field around a building.

One side of the wrapper sprouts an intricate leaf pattern; on the other side, clusters of people are grouped to resemble floating seedpods.

After lengthy experimentation with wrapping techniques, the designers fine-tuned a mathematical folding pattern that follows the Fibonacci sequence (in which the width of each fold is equal to the combined widths of the two preceding folds). When folded, the cover forms pockets in which extra documents can be stored. The cover is attached to the book's spine.

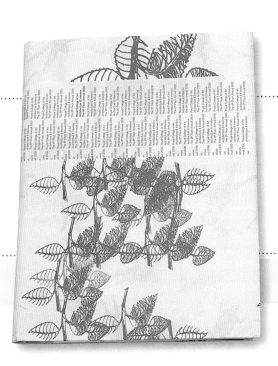

COUNTRIES	France/UK
DESIGN FIRM	EricandMarie
CREATIVE DIRECTORS	Marie Bertholle & Eric Gaspar
DESIGNERS	Marie Bertholle & Eric Gaspar
CLIENT	Royal College of Art
PRINTER	Colortec

COUNTRY	USA
DESIGN FIRM	Gouthier Design
CREATIVE DIRECTOR	Jonathan Gouthier
DESIGNER	Kiley Del Valle
PRINTER	Pfaffco Inc.

Just Their Type

Gouthier Design wanted to showcase its ability to think differently about its clients' brands. The envelope in the firm's stationery system articulates this talent quite eloquently. Although it is a standard policy #10 size (custom cut with a preexisting die), the wallet flap is crisply embellished with a blind embossed *G*. In addition, the firm's name is engraved and its return address is offset printed on the back of the envelope. Each of these typographic elements falls on either side of the envelope's center seam, meaning the job had to be carefully engineered to ensure the type blocks lined up once the envelopes were folded.

It wasn't until after the blind embossed *G* was imprinted on the flaps that Gouthier realized the adhesive company could not apply glue to the envelope flap without ruining the emboss. As a solution, the firm uses glue sticks to seal each envelope by hand. A wraparound, tip-on label flows from front to back and doubles as a decorative fastener. The tip-on proved less costly than printing the striped bar motif on the envelope proper, and it enhances the tactile appeal of each piece of correspondence.

Red Letter Day

The host of this Asian-themed birthday party wished to send a gift to each guest along with the party invitation. Designers at Substância 4 immersed themselves in Eastern philosophy, studying books such as the *I-ching,* to devise a package that was authentic. Various gift items were considered and rejected (including bamboo) before the Chinese lantern was chosen as a symbol of prosperity and enlightenment. As a bonus, the light and compact lanterns collapsed flat for easy delivery by mail.

The party envelope and event invitation are one in the same. An initial envelope prototype constructed of vegetal paper proved too flimsy and was replaced with a sturdier duplex paper that withstood heavy ink coverage on both sides.

COUNTRY	Brazil
DESIGN FIRM	Substância 4
CREATIVE DIRECTORS	Marcia Albuquerque & Carolina Terra
DESIGNERS	Marcia Albuquerque & Carolina Terra
CLIENT	Beth Rebelo
PRINTER	Ano Born

COUNTRY	USA
DESIGN FIRM	And Partners
CREATIVE DIRECTOR	David Schimmel
DESIGNER	David Schimmel
CLIENT	Global Crossing Ltd.
PRINTER	Dickson's

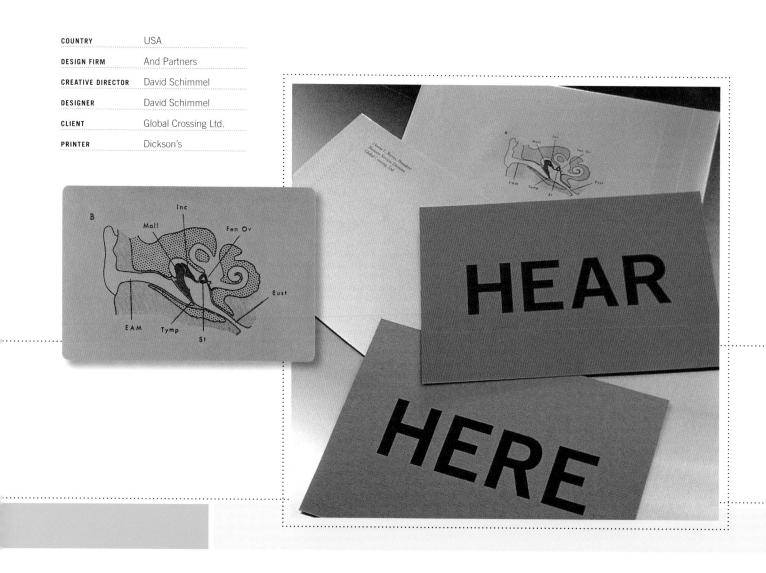

Seen and Heard

Global Crossing, a provider of Internet telecommunications solutions, was inviting a few esteemed guests to an exclusive dinner. The company wanted the invitation envelope to signify something special but stipulated that its own role as event sponsor should remain understated in the presentation.

And Partners created two onomatopoeic cards that discreetly reference the company's core business—communication. The first card ("here") specifies the location of the dinner, while the other card ("hear") highlights the speaker for the evening. Both cards were mailed in a silver matte envelope printed with a medical illustration of the human ear canal. As a departure from the norm, the envelope is perforated along one side (next to the return address label) for easy opening.

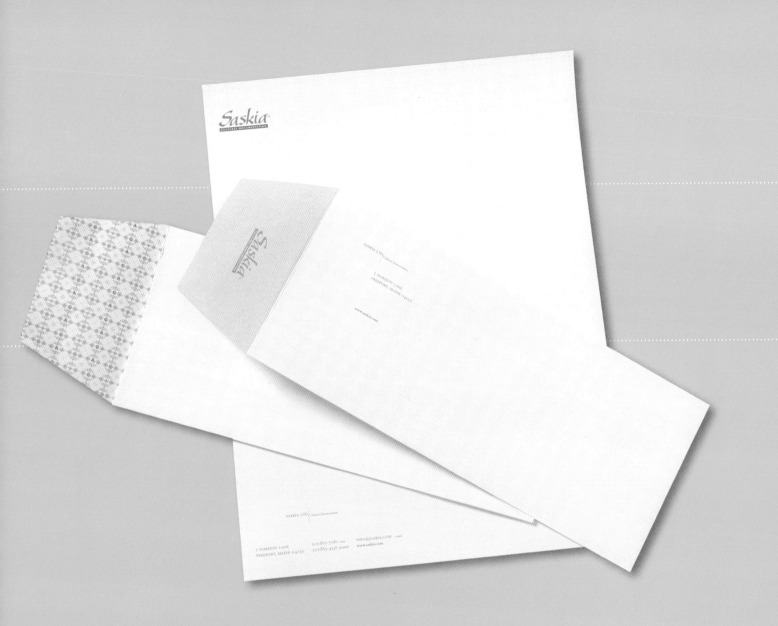

Follow a Pattern

Saskia Ltd. provides digital images of world-famous art collections to art historians for teaching purposes. The company is considered the best in its class, but before 2003, its identity did not match this reputation. Gouthier Design was asked to create a new image for Saskia that reflected its archival quality. The flexible system needed to incorporate a range of materials, including letterhead, envelopes, folders, and inserts that could be custom generated with in-house inkjet printers.

Since Saskia's first impression with university faculty and art historians is typically made through the mail, an elaborate stationery system was apropos. The custom die-cut envelope, used for letters, invoices, and other confidential correspondence, features an eye-catching security pattern that references the company mission. The same pattern is repeated in other marketing materials. The client's business has grown 30 to 40 percent since the redesign, despite a tough economy.

COUNTRY	USA
DESIGN FIRM	Gouthier Design
CREATIVE DIRECTOR	Jonathan Gouthier
DESIGNER	Kiley Del Valle
CLIENT	Saskia Ltd.
PRINTER	Southeastern Printing

COUNTRY	USA / Europe
DESIGN FIRM	General Public
CREATIVE DIRECTOR	Gabe Goldman
PHOTOGRAPHERS	Dennis Wise & Studio Three
CLIENT	Highgear
PRINTER	ColorGraphics

Mod and Modular

Highgear, an outdoor products company, needed a versatile and stylish dealer catalog that could be updated monthly and used in both U.S. and European markets. The catch? The company goes by two different names—depending on the market—but lacked the budget to print sister catalog covers.

The solution, devised by General Public, was to use the mailing envelope proper as a shell housing a set of loose, interchangeable catalog inserts. In this regard, the envelope functions as a vessel to preserve information, as well as a full-bleed catalog "cover" and transportation device. The company brand name, as seen through a die-cut window in the envelope, can be changed with a simple insert.

Recognizing that buyers of Highgear products are urbanites as well as adventure travelers, designer Gabe Goldman cast the goods as rugged fashion accessories. The unorthodox catalog style also makes a strong fashion statement.

Play Ball

Executive recruiting is a competitive playing field. Resources Connection, an international recruiter specializing in finance, accounting, human resources, and information technology stepped up to the plate with style. A marketing piece designed to increase awareness of the firm's services leverages the concept of teamwork. Baseball becomes an effective metaphor for the recruiter's ability to help top execs fill key positions, just as the general manager of a ball team scouts the best talent to fill his roster.

The envelope, constructed of uncoated, cover-weight, flecked stock, unfolds to reveal a rendering of a baseball diamond. The cover flap is die-cut in the shape of home plate. The capacity mailer was sent with a small brochure and a set of baseball trading cards.

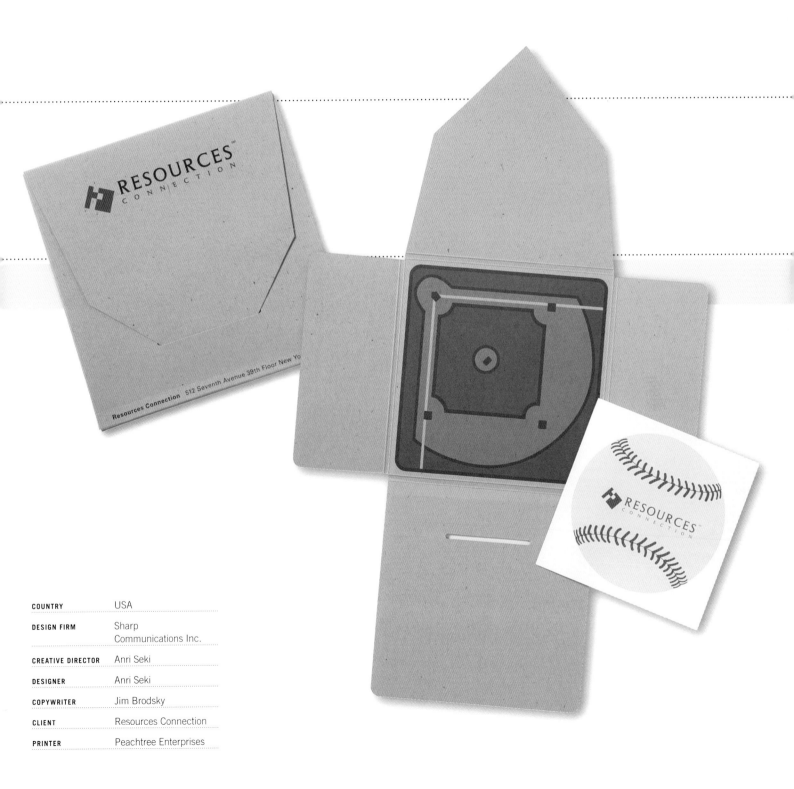

COUNTRY	USA
DESIGN FIRM	Sharp Communications Inc.
CREATIVE DIRECTOR	Anri Seki
DESIGNER	Anri Seki
COPYWRITER	Jim Brodsky
CLIENT	Resources Connection
PRINTER	Peachtree Enterprises

COUNTRY	UK
DESIGN FIRM	Pemberton and Whitefoord Design
CREATIVE DIRECTOR	Simon Pemberton
DESIGNER	Spedding Westrip
COPYWRITER	Simon Rodway
PHOTOGRAPHER	James Murphy
CLIENT	James Murphy
PRINTER	Burlington Press

Fresh Catch

There's something fishy about this promo mailer for James Murphy, a London food photographer. Building on a "fish and chips" theme, designers at Pemberton and Whitefoord conjured up a fictitious maritime newspaper—complete with fish tales and a custom crossword puzzle—to be used as "fish wrap" for an appetizer of Murphy's savory work.

Promo postcards are tucked inside the self-closing newsprint envelope, along with vinegar and salt packets, and a chip fork. The piece sparked a feeding frenzy among new clients.

Check's in the Mail

Designers at Hornall Anderson were so tired of the firm's logo that they ripped down the sign in their lobby. Eventually, the team got around to fine-tuning their identity, making it cleaner and more contemporary.

The logo, a simple iconic morph of the *H* and *A* in the studio's name, sets the tone for a witty stationery system that engages recipients instantly.

Business cards have a fill-in-the-blank element on the back. Envelopes feature check boxes next to statements such as "not a bill" and "may save your life someday." The trick was making sure the type on the envelope flap and body aligned once the envelopes were converted.

COUNTRY	USA
DESIGN FIRM	Hornall Anderson Design Works
ART DIRECTORS	Jack Anderson & John Hornall
DESIGNERS	Jack Anderson, Henry Yui, Andrew Wicklund, & Mark Popich
CLIENT	Hornall Anderson Design Works
PRINTER	Robert Horsely Printing

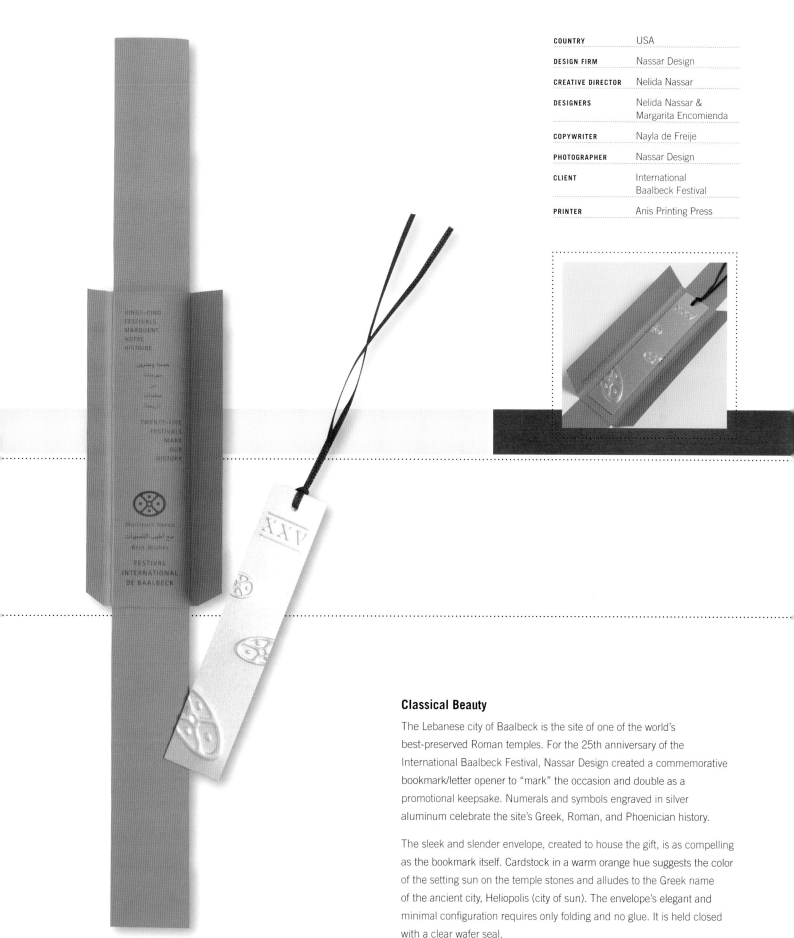

COUNTRY	USA
DESIGN FIRM	Nassar Design
CREATIVE DIRECTOR	Nelida Nassar
DESIGNERS	Nelida Nassar & Margarita Encomienda
COPYWRITER	Nayla de Freije
PHOTOGRAPHER	Nassar Design
CLIENT	International Baalbeck Festival
PRINTER	Anis Printing Press

Classical Beauty

The Lebanese city of Baalbeck is the site of one of the world's best-preserved Roman temples. For the 25th anniversary of the International Baalbeck Festival, Nassar Design created a commemorative bookmark/letter opener to "mark" the occasion and double as a promotional keepsake. Numerals and symbols engraved in silver aluminum celebrate the site's Greek, Roman, and Phoenician history.

The sleek and slender envelope, created to house the gift, is as compelling as the bookmark itself. Cardstock in a warm orange hue suggests the color of the setting sun on the temple stones and alludes to the Greek name of the ancient city, Heliopolis (city of sun). The envelope's elegant and minimal configuration requires only folding and no glue. It is held closed with a clear wafer seal.

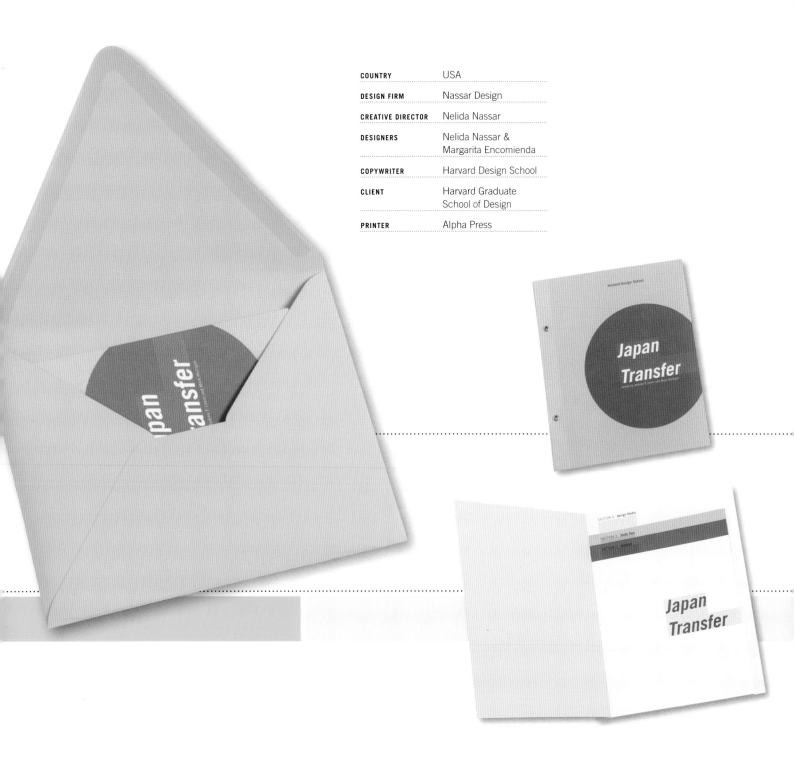

COUNTRY	USA
DESIGN FIRM	Nassar Design
CREATIVE DIRECTOR	Nelida Nassar
DESIGNERS	Nelida Nassar & Margarita Encomienda
COPYWRITER	Harvard Design School
CLIENT	Harvard Graduate School of Design
PRINTER	Alpha Press

A Yen for Simplicity

For an architectural course on Japanese modernism at Harvard Graduate School of Design, Nassar Design was asked to create a publication highlighting various aspects of Tokyo's urban life and culture, as expressed in the city's architecture, planning, landscape design, and history. The publication would ultimately be used as the basis for a Japan Society building in Boston.

Pages in the booklet are cut at different widths and heights to evoke the city's many rich layers, and the minimalist cover references the simplicity of the Japanese flag.

The envelope for the booklet needed to be equally striking, yet spare, so as not to overpower its contents. Taking a cue from the Japanese affinity for tactile elegance, the firm selected a smooth, strong, uncoated hue sheet with a luxurious heft. Whereas standard 9" X 12" (22.5 X 30 cm) envelopes come with square flaps, this one is outfitted with a generous pointed flap. The result is a memorable piece that reads like an oversized invitation.

Bern, Baby, Bern

P_A_R_T is an initiative in Bern, Switzerland, to encourage youth participation in the civic and social life of the city. A plastic zippered mail pouch—purchased off the shelf and customized with a printed label—provides a transparent view of five mix-and-match booklets inside.

Meant to read like a survival kit, the punchy resource offers fresh ideas about everything from political activism to teen counseling, to where to rent a video camera or rehearsal space. A tight budget limited the piece to three ink colors, but overprinting of fluorescent pink and yellow creates the illusion of a five-toned electric palette. A digitized map gives the package a hip, techno vibe.

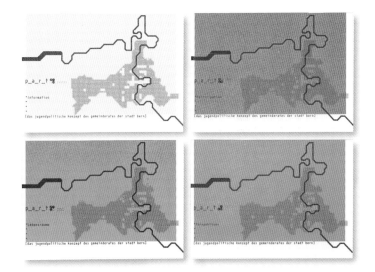

COUNTRY	Switzerland
DESIGN FIRM	superbüro
CREATIVE DIRECTOR	Barbara Ehrbar
DESIGNER	Barbara Ehrbar
COPYWRITERS	Carolin Demeny & Alex Haller
CLIENT	P_A_R_T
PRINTER	Rub Media

COUNTRY	USA
DESIGN FIRM	Juicebox Designs
CREATIVE DIRECTOR	Jay Smith
DESIGNER	Jay Smith
COPYWRITER	Jay Smith
CLIENT	Juicebox Designs
PRINTER	Buford Lewis Printing

Packed with Flavor

Jay Smith could have taken the literal route and incorporated fruit cartoons and zany colors into the identity for Juicebox Designs. Instead, he threw a few retro ingredients into the blender. Referencing the studio's play on the word "jukebox," the uncoated, eggshell stationery evokes an era when full service didn't cost extra. Distressed type and a vintage 1950s palette mix tastily with faux contemporary product labeling.

The custom-converted #10 envelope is a fresh departure from mail pieces past and present. Smith secured USPS approval to print the Juicebox logo as a banner across the top of the envelope. He mailed several handmade dummies to himself as a pretest before the job went into production. A square flap on the back of the envelope accommodates a return address —and the recommended daily allowance of lighthearted sales copy, which echoes their business card design (right).

Atomic Energy

Detector, an alien, robotic font created by designer Mladen Balog for the computer networking giant Verso, makes for an animated CD folder. An outlined version of the typeface is magnified and cropped so that the letterforms read as abstract graphics. A die-cut portion of the letter *o* makes for an unusual interlocking closure that reads like a space age blob. A palette of metallic silver, black, and astral colors completes the theme.

A funny thing about the palette: incorrect PMS numbers were sent to the printer. The final colors were unexpected, but the client liked them anyway.

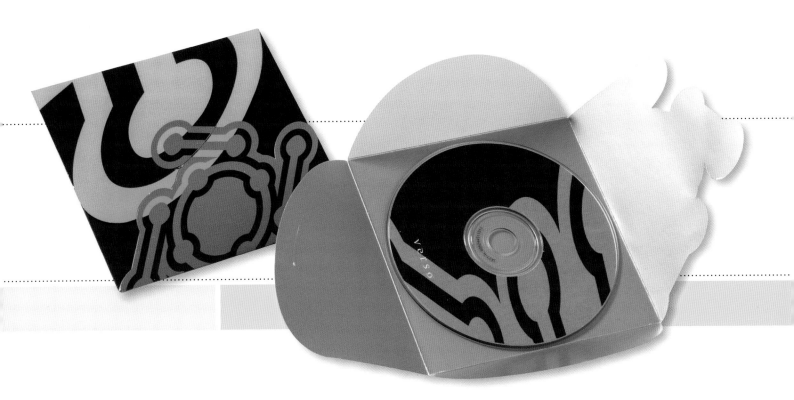

COUNTRY	Croatia
DESIGN FIRM	Likovni Studio
CREATIVE DIRECTORS	Danko Jaksic & Tomislav Mrcic
DESIGNER	Mladen Balog
CLIENT	Verso
PRINTER	Tiskara Kolaric

Quick Fix

General Public is a creative firm specializing in triage. Its brand experts help mend broken communication lines between consumers and products so companies can build equity in their respective retail marketplaces. A semitransparent envelope mimicking the style of first aid packaging forms the crux of the studio's Brand Aid self promo.

The creative team searched for selfsealing, sterile bags to hold its catalog and sticker, but found only versions that required autoclave sealing. Screen-printed vellum was used as an alternative for the envelope, which pulls apart like a Band-Aid wrapper. Several test mailers confirmed that the stock would withstand the rigors of the postal system without becoming damaged. General Public acquired four new accounts after mailing the kit to prospective clients as an icebreaker.

COUNTRY	USA
DESIGN FIRM	General Public
CREATIVE DIRECTOR	Gabe Goldman
CLIENT	General Public
PRINTER	Revolution

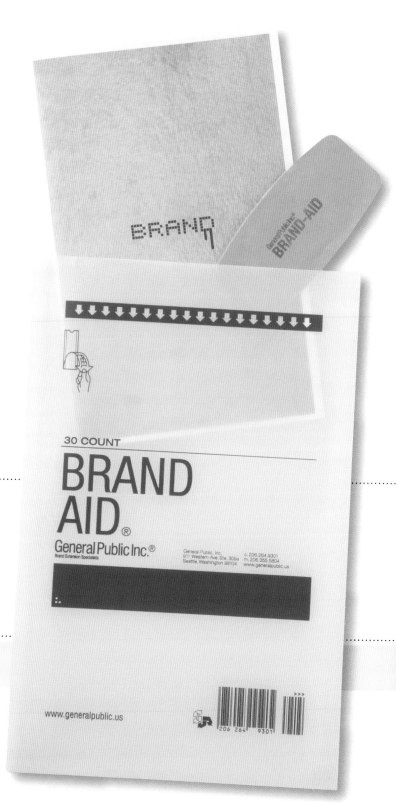

COUNTRY	Switzerland
DESIGN FIRM	superbüro
CREATIVE DIRECTORS	Daniel Zehntner, Werner Rudolf, & Barbara Ehrbar
DESIGNER	Barbara Ehrbar
CLIENT	F. Preisig AG
PRINTER	Feldegg Druckerei/Sonderegger

In the Clouds

F. Preisig AG is a national engineering enterprise in Switzerland. The company's identity system is derived from a toolbox of modular shapes, colors, images, and typography. Collage pieces in the system blend three kinds of elements: the perspective grid represents the logic of the engineer; photographs of water, earth, and sky signify the firm's commitment to ecological stewardship; and finally, abstract, monochromatic shapes represent the engineer's intervention in the natural world.

The whimsical envelope in the firm's stationery system demonstrates the power of montage. A photograph of floating clouds is printed on the inside of the envelope. The puffy, organic shapes peek through the man-made, die-cut window.

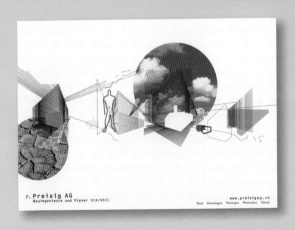

ACTION PRINT
1776 22nd Street
West Des Moines, IA 50266
USA
Tel: 515.226.1776
www.action-print.com

ALPHA PRESS
57 Harvard Street
Waltham, MA 02453-4280
USA
Tel: 781.894.5300

ANIS COMMERCIAL PRINTING PRESS
PO Box 11-2560
Beirut
Lebanon
www.anispress.com.lb

ANO BOM
Av. Presidente Kennedy, 1843
Ano Bom Barrà Mansa RJ 27325-000
Brazil

ART REAL
20 S. Linden Avenue, Suite 4A
South San Francisco, CA 94080-6425
USA
Tel: 650.871.893

ARTES GRAFICA PANORAMA
Avena No. 629
Col Granjas 08400
Mexico

ASAHI SEIHAN PRINTING COMPANY LTD.
1-4-6 Houenzaka, Chuoku
Osaka 540-0006
Japan

AWS DRUCKTECHNIK GMBH
Max-Planck-Str. 5-13
71254 Ditzingen
Germany

BAMBRA PRESS
6 Rocklea Drive
Port Melbourne, Victoria 3207
Australia

BILLINGHAM PRESS LTD.
155 Central Avenue
Billingham TS23 1LF
UK

BRYSON PRINT
21D Oak Road
West Chirton Industrial Estate
Tyne & Wear NE29 8SF
UK

BUFORD LEWIS
1107 8th Avenue S.
Nashville, TN 37203-4723
USA

BURDGE, INC.
2151 Yates Avenue
Los Angeles, CA 90040-1911
USA
Tel: 800.962.2486
Fax: 323.724.7901
www.burdge.com

BURLINGTON PRESS LTD.
Station Road
Foxton
Cambridgeshire CB2 6SW
UK
www.burlingtonpress.co.uk

CENVEO GRAPHIC ARTS CENTER
832 S. Fidalgo Street
Seattle, WA 98108-2616
USA
Tel: 206.767.4190
www.cenveo.com
www.gacnw.com

CHAUCER PRESS
25 Shakespeare Road
PO Box 10079
Waltham, Christchurch
New Zealand
www.chaucer.co.nz

CLASSIC LITHO
340 Maple Avenue
Torrance, CA 90503-2600
USA
Tel: 310.224.5200
Fax: 310.224.5202
www.classiclitho.com

COE DISPLAY
301 22nd Street
Long Island City, NY 11101-5031
USA

COLORGRAPHICS
1421 S. Dean Street
Seattle, WA 98144
USA
Tel: 206.682.7171
www.colorgraphics.com

COLORTEC LTD.
Honywood House
Honywood Road
Basildon Essex SS14 3EN
UK

CONTACT CREATIVE SERVICES INC.
1180 Wilton Grove Road
London, ON N6N 1C8

CREATIVE FINISHING INC.
1 Concord Square #5
Boston, MA 02118-3183
USA

DEJAY LITHO INC.
599 11th Avenue
New York, NY 10036-2110

DICKSON'S
1484 Atlanta Industrial Way NW
Atlanta, GA 30331-1000
USA
www.dicksons.com

DIVERSIFIED GRAPHICS INC.
1700 Broadway Street NE
Minneapolis, MN 55413-2618
USA
Tel: 800.233.7454
Fax: 612.331.1111
www.dgi.net

DONLEVY LITHOGRAPH INC.
729 S. Emporia Street
Wichita, KS 67211-2307
USA

DRUCKEREI DITZEN GMBH & CO. KG
Hafenstrasse 140
27576 Bremerhaven
Germany

DRUCKEREI KOCHWASSER GMBH
Tabaksmühlenweg 30 d
61440 Oberursel
Germany

DRUCKHAUS WÜST GMBH
Weißenberger Strasse 12
27628 Driftsethe
Germany

EVERGREEN QUALITY PRESS
222 S. Orcas Street
Seattle, WA 98108-2441
USA

FELDEGG DRUCKEREI/SONDEREGGER
Zürcherstr. 60
PO Box 1171
5500 Wil
Switzerland

FIELD PRINT
9 Hutton Street Industrial Estate
Boldon Colliery NE35 9LW
UK

FOREMOST GRAPHICS
2921 Wilson Drive NW
Grand Rapids, MI 49544-7565
USA
Tel: 800.728.8775
Fax: 616.453.0505
www.foremostgraphics.com

GF SMITH
11/13 Weston Street
Bermondsey
London SE1 3ER
UK
www.gfsmith.com

GOOD NEWS
Hallsford Bridge
Ongar Essex CM5 9RX
UK

GRAPHIC VISIONS INC.
2860 N. Ontario Street
Burbank, CA 91504-2105
USA

H&D GRAPHICS
950 SE 8th Street
Hialeah, FL 33010-5740
USA
Tel: 800.443.9599

HARTLEY'S PRINTING COMPANY
2 Seaview Units, Lewis Road, Ocean Park
Cardiff CF24 5EB
UK

HFW PLASTICS LTD.
Albany Road
Gateshead NE8 3AT
UK

INDONESIA PRINTER
Jl. Bluit Karang Karya 1
Blok A Utara No. 5–6
Jakarta 14450
Indonesia

INLAND LITHO
4305 E La Palma Avenue
Anaheim, CA 92807-1805
USA
Tel: 714.993.6000
Fax: 714.993.6686
www.inlandlitho.com

KEA INC.
8795 River Heights Way
Inver Grove Heights, MN 55076-3477
USA
Tel: 612.386.216

K/P CORPORATION
2001 22nd Avenue S.
Seattle, WA 98144-4552
USA
Tel: 800.328.3284
Fax: 206.328.4919
www.kpcorp.com

LULU ISLAND PRINTERS
1-11771 Horseshoe Way
Richmond, BC V7A 4V4
Canada

O'NEIL PRINTING
366 N. 2nd Avenue
Phoenix, AZ 85003-1517
USA
Tel: 888.838.5815
Fax: 602.258.4504
www.oneilprint.com

OSCAR PRINTING COMPANY
57 Columbia Square
San Francisco, CA 94103-4015
USA
Tel: 415.626.8818
Fax: 415.626.8828
www.oscarprinting.com

PARAGRAPHICS
123 Mitchell Boulevard
San Rafael, CA 94903-2003
USA
Tel: 415.472.0220

PEACHTREE ENTERPRISES
2219 41st Avenue
Long Island City, NY 11101-4803
USA

PFAFFCO INC.
759 NW 24th Street
Miami, FL 33127-4260
USA
Tel: 305.635.0986
Fax: 305.635.7741
www.pfaffco.com

PICCARI PRESS INC.
315 W. Street Road
Warminster, PA 18974-3208
USA
Tel: 888.455.5090
Fax: 215.442.1901
www.picarri.com

PRINTING INC.
344 N. Saint Francis Street
Wichita, KS 67202-2622
USA

REVOLUTION INC.
421 Fairview Avenue N.
Seattle, WA 98109
USA
Tel: 206.748.0055

ROADRUNNER PRESS
2320 W. Magnolia Boulevard
Burbank, CA 91506-1736
USA
Tel: 818.843.8722

ROBERT HORSLEY PRINTING
108 NW Canal Street
Seattle, WA 98107
USA

RUB MEDIA
Falkenplatz 11
3000 Berne
Switzerland

SOMERSET GRAPHICS COMPANY LTD.
370 Brunel Road
Mississauga, ON L4Z 2C2
Canada
Tel: 866.217.2442
Fax: 905.890.7489
www.somersetgraphics.com

SOUTHEASTERN PRINTING
3601 SE Dixie Highway
Stuart, FL 34997-5246
USA
Tel: 800.226.8221

SPECTRUM PRINTING
3640 Princeton Oaks Street
Orlando, FL 32808-5636
USA
Tel: 407.889.3100
Fax: 407.889.0993
www.spectrumprint.net

TEAM IMPRESSION LTD.
Fusion House
1 Lockwood Close
Leeds LS11 5OU
UK

TISKARA KOLARIC
Poljacka 7 2AGREB
Croatia

TYPECRAFT WOOD & JONES
2040 E. Walnut Street
Pasadena, CA 91107-5804
USA
Tel: 626.795.8093
Fax: 626.795.2423
www.typecraft.com

WOOD MITCHELL PRINTERS LTD.
Festival Way, Festival Park
Stoke on Trent ST1 5TH
UK

YAHALOMI ZISMAN
11B Hayezira Street
PO Box 2452
Raanana 43663
Israel

ZENITH MEDIA
Moy Road Industrial Estate
Taffs Well
Cardiff CF15 7QR
UK

52 PICK-UP INC.
672 Dupont Street
Suite 310
Toronto, ON M6G 126
Canada
Tel: 416.537.5200
Fax: 416.537.5354
www.52pick-up.com
108–109

AFTERHOURS
JL. Merpati Raya 45
Menteng Dalam
Jakarta 12870
Indonesia
Tel: 62.21.8306819
Fax: 62.21.8290612
www.afterhoursgroup.com
94–95

ALOOF DESIGN LTD.
132 Western Road
Lewes
East Sussex BN7 1RR
UK
Tel: 44.1273.470887
www.aloofdesign.com
119

AND PARTNERS, NY
156 Fifth Avenue
Suite 1234
New York, NY 10010
Tel: 212.414.4700
Fax: 212.414.2915
www.andpartnersny.com
120, 142

BAUMANN & BAUMANN
Büro für Gestaltung
Taubentalstraße 4/1
73525 Schwäbisch Gmünd
Germany
Tel: 49.7171.927990
Fax: 49.7171.927999
baumannandbaumann.com
82–83

BBK STUDIO
459 Monroe Avenue NW
Suite 212
Grand Rapids, MI 49503
Tel: 616.459.4444
Fax: 616.459.4477
www.bbkstudio.com
130

BECKER DESIGN
225 East St. Paul Avenue
Suite 300
Milwaukee, WI 53202
Tel: 414.224.4942
Fax: 414.224.4943
www.beckerdesign.net
71

BE DESIGN
1306 Third Street
San Rafael, CA 94901
Tel: 415.451.3530
Fax: 415.451.3532
www.bedesign.net
131

BELYEA
1809 Seventh Avenue
Suite 1250
Seattle, WA 98101
Tel: 206.682.4895
Fax: 206.623.8912
www.belyea.com
10, 15, 17, 19, 20,
20, 22, 24, 31

BLØK DESIGN
Atlixco 50B
La Condesa
Cuauhtemoc
Mexico DF 06140
Tel: 52.55.55.53.5076
Fax: 52.55.55.53.99.97
www.blokdesign@att.net.mx
38, 80, 116–117

BLUELOUNGE DESIGN
32 S. Raymond Avenue
Suite 9
Pasadena, CA 91105
Tel: 626.564.2802
Fax: 626.564.2722
www.bluelounge.com
50–51, 56–57, 98–99

BLUE RIVER DESIGN LTD.
The Foundry
Forty Banks
Newcastle Upon Tyne NE1 3PA
UK
Tel: 0191.261.0000
Fax: 0191.261.0010
www.blueriver.co.uk
47, 114–115

**BRAUE: BRANDING
& CORPORATE DESIGN**
Eiswerkestrasse 8
27572 Bremerhaven
Germany
Tel: 0049.471.983.82.0
Fax: 0049.471.983.82.30
www.braue.info
88, 89

CAVE DESIGN
3500 NW Boca Raton Boulevard
Suite 808
Boca Raton, FL 33431
Tel: 561.417.0780
Fax: 561.417.0490
www.caveimages.com
132

CHEN DESIGN ASSOCIATES
589 Howard Street
Fourth Floor
San Francisco, CA 94105
Tel: 415.896.5338
Fax: 415.896.5339
www.chendesign.com
96–97

COMMUNICATION VISUAL
1627 K Street NW
Fifth Floor
Washington, DC 20006
Tel: 202.463.2367
Fax: 202.822.3650
www.com-vis.com
134

DAVID CARTER DESIGN
4112 Swiss Avenue
Dallas, TX 75204
Tel: 214.826.4631
Fax: 214.827.1938
www.dcadesign.com
62

DOSSIERCREATIVE INC.
402–611 Alexander Street
Vancouver, BC V6A 1E1
Canada
Tel: 604.255.2077
Fax: 604.255.2097
www.dossiercreative.com
36

ELFEN
20 Harrowby Lane
Cardiff Bay
Wales CF10 5GN
UK
Tel: 44.29.2048.4824
Fax: 44.29.2048.4823
www.elfen.co.uk
102–103

ERICANDMARIE
65 Avenue Montaigne
75008 Paris
France
Tel: 0033.1.60.70.93.32
Fax: 0033.1.60.70.93.32
www.ericandmarie.com
76–77, 139

FLIGHT CREATIVE
Studio 14/15 Inkerman Street
St. Kilda, Victoria
Australia 3182
Tel: 613.9534.4690
Fax: 613.9593.6029
www.flightcreative.com
72–73

GENERAL PUBLIC INC.
911 Western Avenue
Suite 305A
Seattle, WA 98104
Tel: 206.264.9301
www.generalpublic.us
144, 154

GILLESPIE DESIGN
32 West 31st Street
Studio 7
New York, NY 10001
Tel: 212.239.1520
Fax: 212.239.1503
www.gillespiedesign.com
118

GOUTHIER DESIGN
2604 NW 54 Street
Fort Lauderdale, FL 33309
Tel: 954.739.7430
Fax: 954.739.3746
www.gouthier.com
140, 143

GRAPHICA
611 Eastlake Avenue East
Seattle, WA 98109
Tel: 206.652.9646
Fax: 206.652.9654
www.graphicasolutions.com
86

GRETEMAN GROUP
1425 E. Douglas
Suite 200
Wichita, KS 67211
Tel: 316.263.1004
Fax: 316.263.1060
www.gretemangroup.com
58–59, 127

**HORNALL ANDERSON
DESIGN WORKS**
1008 Western Avenue
Suite 600
Seattle, WA 98104
Tel: 206.467.5800
Fax: 206.467.6411
www.hadw.com
32–33, 60–61,
74–75, 100–101, 148

IE DESIGN + COMMUNICATIONS
422 Pacific Coast Highway
Hermosa Beach, CA 90254
Tel: 310.376.9600
Fax: 310.376.9604
www.iedesign.net
128, 136–137

**JASON & JASON
VISUAL COMMUNICATION**
118 Hayetzira Street
PO Box 2432
Raanana 43663
Israel
Tel: 972.9.7444282
Fax: 972.9.7444292
www.jasonandjason.com
46, 54, 55, 78–79

JUICEBOX DESIGNS
4709 Idaho Avenue
Nashville, TN 37209
Tel: 615.297.1682
Fax: 615.297.1688
www.juiceboxdesigns.com
152

LIKOVNI STUDIO
Dekanići 42, Kerestinec
10431 Sveta Nedjelja
Croatia
Tel: 385.1.4670.327
Fax: 385.1.4612.015
www.list.hr
153

LLOYDS GRAPHIC DESIGN LTD.
17 Westhaven Place
Blenheim
New Zealand
Tel: 64.3.578.6955
Fax: 64.3.578.6955
112–113

MAIOW CREATIVE BRANDING
Aylesbury House
17–18 Aylesburg Street
Clerkenwell, London EC1R 0DB
Tel: 44.020.7566.0021
Fax: 44.020.7566.0051
www.maiow.com
52–53, 122–123

METHODOLOGIE
808 Howell Street
Suite 600
Seattle, WA 98101
Tel: 206.623.1044
Fax: 206.625.0154
www.methodologie.com
40, 44–45, 84–85

MINALE BRYCE DESIGN STRATEGY
56 Little Edward Street
Spring Hill, Brisbane
Queensland 4000
Australia
Tel: 617.3831.4149
Fax: 617.3832.1653
www.minalebryce.com
65

NASSAR DESIGN
11 Park Street
Brookline, MA 02446
Tel: 617.264.2862
Fax: 617.264.2861
41, 48, 133, 149, 150

NOON
592 Utah Street
San Francisco, CA 94110
Tel: 415.621.4922
Fax: 415.621.4966
www.designatnoon.com
42–43

**PEMBERTON AND
WHITEFOORD DESIGN**
21 Ivor Place
Marylebone, London NW1 6EU
Tel: 44.020.7723.8899
Fax: 44.020.7723.6131
www.p-and-w.com
138, 146–147

PINPOINT COMMUNICATIONS
426 South Military Trail
Deerfield Beach, FL 33442
Tel: 954.574.0601
Fax: 954.574.0609
126

PRANK DESIGN
PO Box 298
Allston, MA 02134
Tel: 617.470.4097
www.prankdesign.com
121

RIORDON DESIGN
131 George Street
Oakville, Ontario L6J 389
Canada
Tel: 905.339.0750
Fax: 905.339.0753
www.riordondesign.com
64, 66, 67, 70, 87

RULE29
821 Kindberg Court
Elburn, IL 60119
Tel: 630.365.5420
Fax: 630.365.5430
www.rule29.com
37, 92–93, 104–105,
106–107, 110–111

SAYLES GRAPHIC DESIGN
3701 Beaver Avenue
Des Moines, IA 50310
Tel: 515.279.2922
Fax: 515.279.0212
www.saylesdesign.com
125

SHARP COMMUNICATIONS INC.
425 West Madison Avenue
New York, NY 10017
Tel: 212.829.0002 x108
81, 135, 145

SHINNOSKE INC.
2-1-8-602 Tsuriganecho
Chuoku, Osaka 540-0035
Japan
Tel: 81.6.6943.9077
Fax: 81.6.6943.9078
www.shinn.co.jp
124

SIMON & GOETZ DESIGN
Westhafen Pier 1
Rotfeder-Ring 11
60327 Frankfurt/Main
Germany
Tel: 49.069.968855.0
Fax: 49.069.968855.23
www.brand-equity-group.com
34–35

SO DESIGN CO.
420 North Fifth Street
Suite 855
Minneapolis, MN 55401
Tel: 612.338.5720
Fax: 612.338.5722
www.sodesignco.com
90–91

STUDIO INTERNATIONAL
Buconjiceva 43, HR-10,000
Zagreb, Croatia
Tel: 385.1.3760.171
Fax: 385.1.3760.172
www.studio-international.com
63

SUBSTÂNCIA 4
Estrada Sorimã
302 Barra da Tijuca
Rio de Janeiro
Brazil 22611-030
Tel: 55.21.2429.3452
Fax: 55.21.2429.3452
www.substancia4.com.br
141

SUPERBÜRO
Dammweg 3
Ch-2502 Biel/Bienne
Switzerland
Tel: 41.032.323.2111
Fax: 41.032.325.5122
www.superbuero.com
68–69, 151, 155

TEMPLIN BRINK DESIGN
720 Tehama Street
San Francisco, CA 94103
Tel: 415.255.9295
Fax: 415.255.9296
www.tbd-sf.com
39, 49, 129

Author Biographies

About Patricia Belyea

Patricia Belyea leads a graphic design firm in Seattle aptly named Belyea. Once an award-winning designer, she now serves as strategic and creative director on client projects. One of her passions is teaching, especially workshops on creativity and brainstorming.

A wife and mother of two, Patricia also has an identical twin sister. Traveling to faraway places with her family is a favorite diversion.

About Jenny Sullivan

Jenny Sullivan writes about graphics, architecture, art, small business, and lifestyle topics. Her work has appeared in *HOW, I.D., Washingtonian,* and other consumer and trade magazines. She is the author of two other design books: *Brochures: Making a Strong Impression*, and *Graphic Design America 3*. She lives in the DC area.